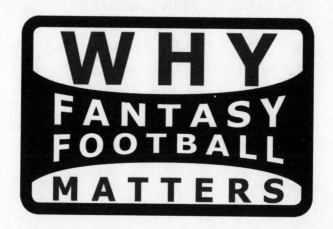

ALSO BY ERIK BARMACK:

THE VIRGIN: A NOVEL

(AND OUR LIVES DO NOT)

ERIK BARMACK AND MAX HANDELMAN

SIMON SPOTLIGHT ENTERTAINMENT
NEW YORK   LONDON   TORONTO   SYDNEY

SIMON SPOTLIGHT ENTERTAINMENT

An imprint of Simon & Schuster

1230 Avenue of the Americas, New York, New York 10020

Text copyright © 2006 by Erik Barmack and Max Handelman

All rights reserved, including the right of reproduction in whole or in part in any form.

SIMON SPOTLIGHT ENTERTAINMENT and related logo are trademarks of Simon & Schuster, Inc.

Designed by Yaffa Jaskoll

Manufactured in the United States of America

First Edition 10 9 8 7 6 5 4 3 2 1

Library of Congress Cataloging-in-Publication Data 2005032414

ISBN-13: 978-1-4169-0996-5

ISBN-10 1-4169-0996-6

<< ACKNOWLEDGMENTS >>

We would first like to thank everyone at Simon Spotlight Entertainment for giving us this opportunity. Specifically, to Tricia Boczkowski for her early support, and the entire marketing and publicity teams—particularly Jen Slattery and Orly Sigal—for their countless hours, thanks very much.

We would like to thank our agent, Byrd Leavell III, whose three-yards-and-a-cloud-of-dust game plan continuously moved the ball forward despite our periodic desire to wildly chuck a Hail Mary or pooch kick it out of bounds. Byrd's passion for the world of fantasy football and guidance through this process was invaluable.

To our real fantasy football brothers in arms—Simon Baukh, Robin Bissell, Jon Brolin, Andrew Grossman, Adam Herzog, David Koshenina, Scott Litman, Jeff Newhams, Basilio "Dubi" Paneque, and Dan Savitt—we thank you for your modicum of decency during this process, useful critiques, and constant flow of good material.

To our parents, thank you for raising such nice young boys. To Elizabeth Banks, your pluckiness is ever appreciated. To Mary Beth Jarrad, you remain an inspiration.

Most of all, to Ryan Fischer-Harbage, a fantastic editor who gets fantasy football even though he cannot fathom ever playing, we thank you for believing in and supporting our project while tolerating our inevitable nonsense.

<< **NOTE TO READERS** >>

Although this book is inspired by our own experiences with fantasy football, none of the managers, incidents, or dialogues described in this book is real.

<< CONTENTS >>

1

<< THE WAR DANCE >>

ALL TRIBES HAVE RITUALS TO PREPARE FOR A NEW SEASON.
Hopi Indians pray for rain, Jews hit the latest Neiman Marcus sale,
Christians make ham and cheese sandwiches, and the Islamic funda-
mentalists dance a jig before showering the sky with gunfire.

Fantasy football tribes are equally devoted to rituals. They take time
and require deep spiritual commitment. A fantasy football fanatic
must be completely dedicated to the season. There's no half-stepping
or wavering. You're either all-in or you're out. And this is specifically
the case in the Bush League—the most competitive and ruthless fantasy football league in the entire western hemisphere.

We prepare for the season. We dance over hot coals. We sing and we
chant, our spears jutting skyward.

We're girding for battle. For our annual rebirth.

JULY 11 THE FLARE ACROSS THE DESERT SKY

The darkest day of the year for any male sports fan.[1] The NBA finals
have just ended, and the pennant races haven't started yet. Tumbleweeds

---

1. We specifically denote "male" sports fan, for had we included females, they might have responded
with some rubbish about the WNBA or a defense of Bikram "hot" yoga.

blow across the barren sports landscape. But all of that is about to change with just one e-mail: *"Subject: Bush League—It's on, gentlemen, it's on."*

The author of this missive is Prashun Thind, pesky Bush League manager extraordinaire. He's hunched over his keyboard, tapping away, ready to get things rolling.

> **Prashun Thind (aka "Prash"):** Manager of the Thindianapolis Colts. A Wall Street investment banker. Resembles a gecko, with dark purple eyelids that remain one-quarter closed. Many think that this look is the result of work fatigue. Actual cause is routine pot smoking. Tends to keep his bony hands perpetually clasped, Mr. Burns–like. Speaks authoritatively on all things statistical.

"Yo, hoes," Prash writes in his e-mail, a flare across the black desert sky. *"Are you bitches ready to throw down? After being stopped short at the goal line last season, the Thindianapolis Colts are now primed for a title run. Team manager, Thindy Infante, has rallied the troops. We're ready, we're primed. Let's get it on."*

Once Prash starts trash-talking, Bush League managers leave their cover. They rub their eyes amid the glimmering light. Just one e-mail and the primal instincts return. The muscles start twitching. The brain starts churning. The fingers start tapping. Preseason has officially begun.

JULY 11 | RALLYING THE TROOPS

Al Lopez shakes his head and grins. He hasn't heard from Thind in seven months. Lopez has little in common with the guy, and has a difficult time discussing anything with him *other* than fantasy football. But looking out his Beverly Hills office window, he has to admit—he misses the little bugger.

> **Al Lopez (aka "El Matador"):** Manager of The Cuban Missile Crisis. A William Morris film agent. In good shape with good teeth and good hair, and decked out in an obligatory

three-button Armani. He's also the lone married guy of the group, and now has a son. Some question whether he can maintain his panache amid the turbulence of fatherhood.

Lopez buzzes his assistant. "Hold all my calls." With that, he enters the fray: *Gentlemen, Prash's standard nonsense aside, I couldn't be more psyched for another season. I've donned my Under Armour, I've stretched my hamstrings. I hope everyone's as fired up as I am. Viva la Bush League!"*
"Here! Here!" writes one manager.
"When are we determining draft order?" asks another.
The Bush League is buzzing.

PRESEASON RITUALS

1. Clear post–Labor Day schedule for draft.
2. Make idle threats about "booting" inactive managers.
3. Watch NFL Films' year in review marathon.
4. Send out e-mail that begins, *"As a former champion . . ."*
5. Participate in an all-rookie dynasty mock draft.

JULY 11 | THE CHECK'S IN THE MAIL

Kwame Jones, the Bush League Commissioner, reads these e-mails, expects more to hit his inbox, and immediately thinks, *Time to get organized.*

Kwame Jones (aka "Kwame Jones"): Manager of Kwame Jones, Inc. A former Purdue University tight end. Now teaches at a Catholic high school. Sports a blue blazer, khakis, and a freshly shaved head. People want Kwame to be hip-hop, but he's much more jazz. Calm, serene. But mess with Kwame and you risk a swift beat-down, though never before he warns: "Dude, you must chill."

"Fellas, let's try to avoid a repeat of last year and get the league entry fees settled up front. Please send me your money. Now."

He immediately receives the first of several hollow promises for quick payment. *"Roger that, Kwame. The proverbial check is in the proverbial mail."*

JULY 15 | SURFING THE MESSAGE BOARDS

In preparation for the upcoming draft in fifty-three days, John Schlotterbeck bookmarks his favorite fantasy football sites. Fanball.com, Footballguys.com, RotoWire.com—he's checking them all. In the background Norman Greenbaum's "Spirit in the Sky" plays loudly over his tinny speakers. Schlots nods his head to the beat as he methodically reviews Tight End rankings.

John Schlotterbeck (aka "Schlots"): Manager of the The Fat Minnesota Guys. Once thin and good-looking, he's now lost much of his hair, grown a sizable paunch, and added an obligatory goatee. He dons a dirty white Notre Dame baseball hat and a purple Minnesota Vikings jacket. He's a midwestern guy: decent, religious, and genuine in all ways. Which makes his divorce from his college sweetheart, Debby Dwaynes, all the more tragic.

"Hey-oh!" Schlots says, giving himself a high five. He's just discovered his first sleeper of the new season.

ON SLEEPERS

A sleeper is an undervalued player with "extreme upside" who's available in the later rounds of a fantasy football draft. Or at least that's the theory. The problem is, guys like Schlots spend so much time hunting for sleepers that by the time the draft has arrived, the players are surprises no longer.

Sifting through Internet message boards, Schlots has "locked in" on an athletic tight end who finished last season with a pair of 100-yard games. Swelling with pride, he e-mails Lopez: *"Al, good buddy, I've found my diamond in the rough."*

"A tight end?" Lopez responds. *"You're a day late and a dollar short. I scouted that guy already."*

Never mind that Lopez hasn't even cracked a fantasy football guide, or started trolling message boards. He has to pretend that he knows everything. *"That guy will be gone by the seventh round. Trust me."*

ALL-TIME BUSH LEAGUE SLEEPERS

1. Clinton Portis, 2002 (1,872 yards, 17 TDs), eighth round
2. Randy Moss, 1998 (1,313 yards, 17 TDs), ninth round
3. Rich Gannon, 2002 (4,698 yards, 27 TDs), seventh round
4. Terrell Owens, 2000 (1,451 yards, 13 TDs), fifth round
5. Stephen Davis, 1999 (1,405 yards, 17 TDs), tenth round

ALL-TIME BUSH LEAGUE NONSLEEPER SLEEPERS

1. Onterrio Smith, 2003 (smoked ganja, split time with Moe Williams), fourth round
2. Michael Vick, 2001 (44.2 completion percentage), third round
3. Charles Rogers, 2003 (243 yards, 3 TDs), fifth round
4. Kellen Winslow, 2004 (50 yards, 0 TDs), sixth round
5. Any Cleveland Browns running back, first through sixteenth rounds (although, with the emergence of Rueben Droughns in the City by the Lake, this trend may now be over, or at least temporarily delayed)

Twelve teams anxiously prepare for the draft. Schlots writes, *"I love Peyton Manning this year, but only late in the first."* Lopez swears that no matter which draft position he gets he's taking two straight running backs. Kwame wants to nab Daunte Culpepper in the second round, but only if he's sure that "his boy" will be there in the third.

The Bush League, in short, has entered full preseason machination mode.

But there's only so much speculating, posturing, and counter-posturing that can happen in a vacuum. The twelve-team draft order must be determined. Who will get the Golden First Pick? And who will get leveled with the Kiss of Death Eleventh Pick?

To assign draft order most leagues drop names in a hat and then select at random. That would be easy. That would make sense. But that would also be boring, and the Bush League won't settle for that.

No, this league uses a far more exotic process. Some have called it barbaric, and others have suggested that it's in poor taste. "Tell that to Saddam Hussein," says Chris O'Brien. No one quite understands his point, but most nod in agreement.

> **Chris O'Brien (aka "The Mick"):** Manager of the Irish Potato Famine. An "e-commerce manager," whatever that means. Rrefers to himself in the third person as "The Mick," which tends to irritate others. Has fiery red hair, and freckles that blot his face when he gets angry. Which happens often. In his book, he's getting screwed. Always. And someone's gotta pay.

"Thind, let's get on with it," O'Brien says. "Some fish are going to have to be sacrificed—it's just that simple."

"Gotcha, O'Brien," Thind says.

Prash has been waiting all summer for the Draft Order Ceremony. Filled with childish glee he heads to a pet store in Chinatown, where he buys twelve goldfish. Each is distinctly different. Some believe this isn't possible, but as it turns out, goldfish come in a variety of shapes, sizes, and colors.

Managers are then assigned fish and asked to name them. Thind calls his POW Fish. Schlots calls his Shaolin Fish. Kwame calls his Kwame Fish. Lopez calls his *El Pescadito.* And Chris O'Brien calls his McFish.

The goldfish are placed in small ziplock bags. Swimming in sharp two-inch arcs, they're taken to Thind's office, where they await their fate.

JULY 19 TAPPING THE TANK

"Gentlemen," Thind e-mails, *"preparations for the Draft Order Ceremony have begun. I haven't fed my two piranhas, Tarkanian and Peepers, for thirty-six hours. Further, I have repeatedly agitated them by tapping on the glass of the tank. I have no doubt that they will make quick work of our twelve little friends."*

JULY 20 THE VOICE OF REASON

Adam Goldman sends out a note urging his fellow Bush Leaguers to abandon the "brutal Draft Order Ceremony."

Adam Goldman: Manager of Team Goyim. The ambivalent Bush League member. Engaged to Margaret Ming, a public relations consultant who supposedly once slept with Puff Daddy. Goldman wears khakis and polo shirts and is prone to leaving Sharpies in his shirt pocket. He's finishing his medical training, with an eye toward becoming a podiatrist. Biggest test, however, is balancing the pressures of the fantasy football season with his fiancée's relentless wedding planning.

"Please, guys, let's find a more humane method." Goldman is roundly mocked. His fish, which he'd begrudgingly called Jew Fish, is renamed Richard Simmons Fish.

Goldman won't relent. *"Last night,"* he writes, *"I had a dream of twelve goldfish screaming. How can you live with that?"*

Schlots replies, *"Goldfish have short memories. If they were in pain last night, they've forgotten it by now."*

JULY 20 ANOTHER VOICE OF REASON

"These guys are a bunch of retards," writes The Death Maiden, as she forwards the goldfish exchange to her colleague at work.

> **The Death Maiden:** Manager of The Dolce and Gabanas. The lone female in the league. Always underestimated, she excels by avoiding the chest-thumping male antagonism prevalent throughout the rest of the league. Much to the consternation of other managers, The Death Maiden has made the play-offs two out of the last three years.

"My God!" her friend answers. *"They really kill goldfish for sport? Remind me again why you're doing this? These guys are total morons."*

"I never get involved in the sideshow," The Death Maiden answers. *"I just love fantasy football, and this is the only competitive league I could get into. They're a good group of guys, but boys will be boys."*

JULY 20 THE GREAT GOLDFISH MASSACRE

Thind opens the double door to his company's conference room, revealing an enormous aquarium. In that aquarium lurk two lethal piranhas—the aforementioned Peepers and Tark. Peepers is pale and speedy; Tark is darker and more of a bruiser. They're the Stockton and Malone of piranhas.

A few minutes before the start of the ceremony, the on-site Bush League managers enter the conference room and take their seats.

Hoping for a last-minute stay of execution, Goldman calls Thind to talk some sense. But Thind merely places him on speakerphone for the amusement of others.

"Such meaningless violence," Goldman says.

"You've called too late," says Thind.

"We can just pick numbers."

"I'm afraid that won't work, Adam. It's over."

"But . . ."

"There's nothing you can do." Thind hangs up.

There's a palpable silence as all eyes focus on the piranhas.

"Bring the pain," commands O'Brien.

Thind drops the twelve goldfish into the tank. The order in which they're eaten will determine the Bush League draft positions. The owner of the first fish consumed will receive the last pick in the draft. The owner of the last fish swimming, the first pick.

The carnage begins quickly. Peepers instantly devours a slow-moving fish before turning his attention to O'Brien's baby.

"Looks like you might have problems there," Schlots says.

O'Brien yells, "Swim, McFish, swim!" But Peepers chases McFish into a toy castle where Tark locks down on him. There's a murky cloud of red, then little McFish scales sink to the bottom of the tank.

O'Brien's goldfish is the second to be consumed. So he's assigned the second to last draft pick—the eleventh pick. This is not, nor will it ever be, a good draft position. O'Brien is furious. "Hey, you gave me a defective fish. The Mick was given a defective fish."

"Here we go with the third-person talk again. O'Brien, stop making excuses. Your fish was torn asunder. And that is that," Thind says.

O'Brien flops his hand. As he leaves the conference room, he shouts, "The Mick knows it's rigged—it's all rigged."[2]

Now there's hooting and hollering as five men press their faces to

2. The Mick is a big believer in conspiracy theories. He thinks that the Patrick Ewing draft lottery was rigged because David Stern wanted a dominant franchise in New York, and he thinks that Michael Jordan's father was gunned down because of gambling debts. He refuses to accept, however, that the WWE is scripted, citing the "fake but competitive theory."

the glass as the carnage unfolds. The water becomes rose-tinted. Half a tail rests inside a plastic treasure chest.

With each new victim, an owner's name is called, and his draft pick assigned. Grown men cheer on small, scrappy goldfish as they dart around the tank trying to avoid the Peepers and Tark killing machine. So it goes until all twelve goldfish are gone and the draft order is set.

MORE COMMON METHODS FOR DETERMINING DRAFT ORDER

1. Random drawing from hat
2. Online number generator
3. Reverse order from previous year's record
4. All-night Texas Hold 'Em poker tourney
5. Bidding for draft slots

JULY 22 CHASING DOWN LEAGUE DUES

"*Guys,*" Kwame writes, "*I still don't have league dues from many of you. I don't want anyone backing out if you're unhappy with your draft spot.*"

The Mick asks if he can get a discount because of his lousy draft position.

Kwame doesn't respond.

JULY 23 ON MOCK DRAFTING

Much as law students conduct mock trials in preparation for real trials (or as practice for editing reams of documents, as the vast majority of these sad saps will), fantasy football managers mock draft.

This is how Schlots is spending most of his summer. He's trying to discover what players will be available to him at his draft spot. Will Clinton Portis slide to him in the first? Will Donovan McNabb be there in the second? And how far will his sleeper fall? Schlots keeps mocking, finding different answers to these questions on a daily basis.

Of course much of this mocking is pointless. You can't predict the way men will act on draft day. Well, actually, you can: competitively, boorishly, and drunkenly. So to put it more precisely: Mock drafts won't get you any closer to understanding the strategies of your rivals.

A mock draft is to fantasy football what the Maginot Line was to World War II—an ineffective defensive barrier. As you may recall, this didn't work out so well for *les grenouilles*. The Germans pump-faked, stutter-stepped through Belgium, and then blitzkrieged into Paris. If World War II can be viewed as a football game— and indeed it can—the Germans circumventing the Maginot Line was like a wide receiver beating a cornerback on a stop-and-go route.

A guy like Schlots is convinced that mock drafting will somehow prepare him for the real draft, or *"la fiesta gordita,"* as he calls it. So he logs many, many hours online, planning speciously, hopping from mock draft to mock draft.

JIBBER-JABBER HEARD IN MOCK DRAFTS

1. *"Kevan Barlow at 2.01? Great upside."*
2. *"I wanted to take Peyton here, but my VBD program told me to take Hines Ward instead."*
3. *"I'm solid at RB1 and RB2. Now it's time to gamble."*
4. *"I smell a tight end run coming on."*
5. *"Brett Favre in the early third round? How can I join your league?"*

AUGUST 5 | ENTER THE DRAGON

Lopez has locked in on his first-round choice. *"It isn't obvious, but it will win me a championship."* Paraphrasing Bruce Lee, he adds, *"It's like a finger, pointing at the moon. If you stare at the finger, you miss all the heavenly glory."* Thind follows up with an e-mail about a new *"value-based drafting algorithm."* Nine out of twelve Bush Leaguers delete both e-mails without opening them.

MOST OVERUSED QUOTES USED IN PRESEASON E-MAILS

1. Michael Corleone: "Just when I thought I was out, they pull me back in."
2. Darth Vader: "The emperor does not share your optimistic appraisal of the situation."
3. Howard Beale: "I'm mad as hell, and I'm not going to take it anymore!"
4. Lawrence of Arabia: "No prisoners! No prisoners!"
5. Alfred Hitchcock: "Revenge is sweet and not fattening."

AUGUST 8 | UP AROUND THE BEND

The Mick is still venting about the Goldfish Ceremony. He hates his eleventh pick in the draft and keeps dwelling on McFish's sub-par performance. "That frickin' fish had no fight—he *wanted* to get eaten."

"True that," Schlots says.

"Now I'm screwed. Totally screwed."

"Sounds about right." Schlots tells O'Brien that he'll "need to reach." According to his mock drafts, the tier-one running backs will be off the board by the time O'Brien picks. The Mick objectively knows that Schlots is right, but he occasionally goes deep into denial and argues that his pick "isn't that bad."

"Isn't that bad?" Schlots says. "Both you and I know that you're up around the bend." Schlots has never used this phrase before, but somehow he instinctively knows that it will annoy the hell out of O'Brien.

O'Brien responds by boasting that he's "bullish" about his position, then admitting that he's screwed, and then feigning enthusiasm again before finally falling into a dreamlike trance.

"The Mick sees it all," he says, referring to himself in rapper-ish third person. "The Mick sees everything falling as it should."

AUGUST 11 | KNOWING YOUR BYE WEEKS

Thind writes, *"I just wanted to let you know that Minnesota and Seattle share the same bye week this year. Keep that in mind."* Kwame crafts a sarcastic e-mail in response and is about to send it—but then he realizes that Thind's right. Of course he's right. Considering bye weeks is pretty damned important.

UNDERRATED PRESEASON ANALYSIS

1. Strength of Schedules
2. Bye-Week Overlaps
3. Offensive Line Breakdowns
4. Third-Year Wide Receiver "Upside" Lists
5. Contract Year "Motivation" Lists

AUGUST 13 | AWAKEN, RIP VAN WINKLE

The NFL preseason commences, and with it the first opportunity for fantasy managers to begin scouting sleepers. Schlots attends a New York

Jets–Detroit Lions game. It's an ugly, ugly affair. But Schlots thinks he's found a "Rip" (that is, a Rip van Winkle, or "sleeper") when a spry second-year wide receiver rolls up serious yards after the catch. Schlots jots the player's name down in his notepad and puts an asterisk next to the name. He then circles the asterisk, and traces the name with a green highlighter.

AUGUST 15 | TRADING DRAFT PICKS

The Mick contacts every member of the Bush League to discuss his draft position. He claims that he loves his pick, but he actually hates it. He can't assemble a competitive team if he's drafting "up around the bend," and he knows it.

Still, he tries to persevere. Each day he considers a new player. First it's Corey Dillon, then it's Terrell Owens, and then it's the massively overhyped Kevan Barlow. But these names are dismissed as quickly as they're considered.

Frantic, O'Brien dials Lopez in LA. "Hey, buddy, how are you—"

"I don't want it—"

"You don't want what?"

"What you're offering."

"And what's that?"

"I don't want anything to do with it," Al says, and then he hangs up.

AUGUST 16 | PUTTING RIP BACK TO BED

Schlots's boy, the "Rip" he'd discovered just days before, goes down with a torn ACL. He's out for the year. Schlots whips out his "scouting book," crosses out the player's name, and writes "injury prone" next to it.

AUGUST 17 | MOCKING THE LATE THIRD ROUND

Schlots and O'Brien are mock drafting again over AOL Instant Messenger. Based on equal parts paranoia and self-amusement, Schlots taunts O'Brien with the claim that *"not a single legitimate running back will be left for you. Not a one."*

Attempting to control his anger, O'Brien closes out his Instant Message window only to see another flashing message from Schlots. He can't help himself—he has to open it. Schlots has reached the end of the third round in their latest mock draft, and he's typed, *"3.11— Jerome Bettis? Marcel Shipp?"*

Furious and trembling, O'Brien logs out. He mutters to himself, "It's not that bad. My draft position is *not* that bad."

AUGUST 18 ENTER THE SANDMAN

"I'm expecting bad things for you all this season, and am keeping careful tabs on your drafting tendencies." So writes The Bitter Drafter, who clocks in with his annual preseason e-mail. His purpose is to put everyone on edge, to establish his loose-cannon bona fides.

> **The Bitter Drafter:** A veritable ghost in the machine. A man whom other managers barely know. How did he get here? And why? The Newman of the Bush League.

"Some of you ridiculed me for taking Jeff Garcia in the second round last year, and that has not been forgotten. I'll show no mercy in drafting your stud players' backups, and will do so to the detriment of my team. I look forward to it, in fact. That's what I do. Carry on."

AUGUST 18 THE NUMBERS GAME

As he does every year, Goldman e-mails Kwame requesting the immediate termination of The Bitter Drafter's Bush League franchise. Kwame responds, as he always does, that the league needs The Bitter Drafter to round out the required twelve managers.

"It's a numbers game," he writes. *"There's nothing I can do."*

O'Brien reaches a tentative agreement to trade his first, third, fifth, tenth, twelfth, and fourteenth picks (plus twenty free-agent dollars and the right to swap backup kickers) to the ever-clueless Two-Headed Hydra for their first, fourth, fifth, sixth, ninth, and eleventh picks.

> **The Two-Headed Hydra (aka "the Guppies"):** A fantasy team run by two guys, usually in an inexperienced, disorganized, and haphazard fashion. By midyear they're likely to hemorrhage good players to other teams in a frustrating, league-altering fashion.

"So what do you say?" says The Mick. "Are we good?"

"I think we're good," says one of the two guys (The Mick isn't sure which). "We just need to chat about it a bit more. We'll get back to you ASAP."

"All right," The Mick says. "Just don't take too long."

"Okay."

"Because I have other offers on the table."

"Right! We're all over it."

The Mick tells them that he's excited to be "creating mutual value dynamics." Then he crunches through another set of player projection models. *Yes,* he thinks, *I've finally climbed out of the hole.*

But before the trade is consummated, Lopez catches wind of the deal. Without really thinking through the ramifications of this trade, he tells The Guppies that they're "giving up incredible value."

"You really think so?" one of them asks.

"Fellas, you're getting hosed."

The Guppies get cold feet and back out.

Through multiple league sources, O'Brien hears about Lopez's tampering. He calls Al a "meddling Hollywood busybody." He then files a formal protest with Kwame, citing Lopez's "interference in all fair trades, and general Drew Rosenhaus–like behavior." Kwame, puzzled and tired, denies that any wrongdoing has occurred.

Goldman declares that the draft date no longer works for him, a date that has been set in stone since the Goldfish Massacre. "I just don't think I can make this work. I'm sorry, but I'm going to have to pass on the Bush League this year."

"Wait—can you work your schedule around Labor Day?"

"No, I have a podiatry conference."

"What about September sixth?"

"Sorry, fellas—no can do. Margaret's dragging me to a baby shower."

"Well what about Wednesday the eighth?"

"Meetings."

Goldman must be boxed in. At first reason is employed: "Could you please give us three or four dates that work?" When he refuses, guilt is applied: "Eleven other guys can make this time. Why can't you?" And then, finally, there's sheer anger: "Dude, do you want to play or not? Because we really can't tell anymore."

Goldman won't budge.

And that's when Al Lopez springs into action. He's like Forrest Gump dashing into the jungle to retrieve a soon-to-be legless Lieutenant Dan. With his persistent, speedy cadence, he tells Adam that everyone's counting on him—that he belongs back in the fray.

Finally Adam concedes.

REASONS WHY MANAGERS LEAVE THE BUSH LEAGUE

1. To spend time with family
2. Embroiled in trade controversy from last season
3. Asked to leave due to late-season inactivity
4. Feigned "work-related" stress
5. Consistent losing record leads to indifference

AUGUST 25 | SPORTSCENTER EXPOSES A SLEEPER

Kwame's convinced that a rookie running back for the Titans will break out by week three of the regular season. He watches the San Francisco–Tennessee preseason game to get a final look at his valuable sleeper. He's quickly devastated, however, when said rookie shakes loose in the first quarter and romps for a 60-yard touchdown. This is a play that's sure to make SportsCenter.

And with that highlight, his sleeper disappears.

AUGUST 26 | FLIGHT RISK

The Mick, a notorious cheapskate, still hasn't paid his league dues. Kwame and others are concerned.

"The Mick could be a flight risk," notes Prashun.

The Mick may bolt the league rather than cough up his hundred-and-fifty-dollar entry fee for a draft spot that he's convinced is "untenable." Kwame informs The Mick that he's set up a PayPal account to make it easy for all managers to "do the right thing."

The Mick, by way of e-mail, claims that his Internet service at work is down, but he'll get "right on it." He won't end up paying his dues until week eight of the regular season.

AUGUST 26 | THE COMMISIONER'S FINAL NOTICE

From: Kwame Jones
Sent: Wednesday, August 25, 2004 1:15 PM
To: Bush League Mailing List
Subject: Be ready, people, be ready

Gentlemen (and Lady):
I just want to confirm that our draft will be held a week

from tomorrow. It will be sixteen rounds of mayhem, followed by two mandatory rounds of backup kickers and defenses. Don't try anything fancy.

Bring your cheat sheets, your depth charts, and your bye-week breakdowns. But Lopez, for God's sake, don't bring your blinding Dolphin's jersey. And, Prashun, this year no Colts foam fingers will be allowed in the War Room.

That is all,

The Commish

2

<< THE LIMBERING-UP E-MAIL >>

From: Prashun Thind
Sent: Thursday, August 26, 2004 3:09 PM
To: Bush League Mailing List
Subject: Limbering Up

Bitches and Hoes:

I thought that it would be useful to bring everyone up to speed on the rest of the Bush League, their mental state or lack thereof, and some plot points to look for as we head toward the draft.

Please note that none of these analyses were conducted scientifically, but rather represent a loose set of observations or outright fiction. In certain instances I have skipped managers entirely because you're simply not worth my time; for years, you have floated around the Bush League and contributed nothing—no good stories, no championships, and very little sustenance for Peepers and Tark. For those who merit my attention, your description is presented according to your draft pick number.

Hope everyone is fired up for the draft. As usual, you best come with it.

Prashun Thind, Busch League Scribe

#1 - Adam Goldman: Mr. Lucky, or Mr. Unlucky, as the case might be. Dr. Goldman has "earned" the #1 pick two years in a row. Now he's hunched over his computer, anxiously chewing his fingernails in a sheer and utter panic as he recalls the last time he had the #1 pick. That year his team collapsed in a heap under the injury-plagued weight of Marshall Faulk, Charles Rogers, and Charlie Garner. Could it happen again?

#2 - Prash: Still puzzled. How could a team that had the best QB (Manning) and one of the best RBs (Tomlinson) last year be so underwhelming? Curious whether anyone cares that his team has had the most points scored *against him* in two of the past three years; fairly sure no one does.

#4 - Kwame Jones: Gliding silently through the water like a tiger shark, waiting to see who he'll gobble up in the first round. Wondering if Priest Holmes is really going to fall to him at #4—just like a few years ago when he ran roughshod over the league. The similarities are eerie. Somebody stop this man before it's too late. Seriously.

#6 - Schlots: Assessing the value of cornering the market on all seven Minnesota running backs, including, but not limited to, Robert Smith, Herschel Walker, and Senator Norm Coleman.

#7 - The Bitter Drafter: Likely putting the finishing touches on his appeal to change the Bush League draft charter, which would reduce the draft from sixteen rounds to five rounds, or to the point when he no longer knows which players to draft, whichever comes first. If his appeal fails, he's openly threatening to vulture at least four backups in the first eight rounds.

#9 - The Death Maiden: Suffering through serious hand cramps after the teacher forced her to write "There is no such thing as beginner's luck" on the chalkboard a hundred times; feeling the pressure to show that last year, drafting with her eyes closed from the #3 spot, was no fluke.

#10 - El Matador: Limbering up for the inevitable close quarters, Sunni-insurgency-style pitched battle that he and The Mick will wage, drafting from the #10 and #11 spots—and the ensuing first weeks of the season, when these two used-car salesmen will kick around a series of trades that will never happen. These are *the* two slots to watch throughout the draft. Al has already determined that should O'Brien select Fred Taylor in the first round, he'll take LaBrandon Toefield at least a round earlier than he should go. Because that's how Al rolls.

#11 - The Mick: Telling anyone who will listen that he loves—LOVES!—his #11 pick, while simultaneously canvassing the league, exploring whether he can trade his pick. Guaranteed to love, then hate, then love, then quit on, then get really excited about, then definitively quit on, his team—all in the span of the first four weeks of the season.

#12 - The Two-Headed Hydra: Belongs at the end of the draft, at the snake position. Inexplicably poring over 2003 mock drafts and trying to reconcile just "Who is this so-called Trung Candidate? Why do we see him going in the late second/early third round? And would pairing him with Tyrone Wheatley be a good or bad thing?" Hoping it can't get any worse than last season. Wait, they have the twelfth pick in the draft, and an inevitable date with Kevan Barlow. So, yes, yes it can.

<< THE DRAFT >>

"Know your enemy and know yourself; in a hundred battles, you will never be defeated."—Sun Tzu, *The Art of War,* ca. 500 B.C.

A SUCCESSFUL DRAFT GOES BEYOND SELECTING THE BEST players. You must also understand your fellow drafters. They're your enemies, and they all have specific strengths, weaknesses, and buttons to be pushed. Knowing their drafting tendencies will put you at a distinct advantage.

But to do so requires understanding the profound psychodynamics of fantasy football. We've spent countless hours diagramming the personalities of our fellow Bush League managers, and we believe that among all the different, zany, and unpredictable drafters out there, consistencies can be found. Patterns emerge. And, if you concentrate hard enough, even the savviest drafter becomes predictable.

THE OUT-OF-DATE CHEAT SHEET DRAFTER

The Out-of-Date Cheat Sheet Drafter is a peasant thrown to the lions for our amusement. He means well, has a good heart, and tries in earnest. But a man is only as good as his weaponry, and this guy has come armed with a meager slingshot and pebbles.

And the inevitable result of this flaccid bit of drafting artillery often leads to his selecting a retired, cut, or injured player. Remarkably, that guy is often Ricky Watters. We can't explain why.

PLAYERS TAKEN BY THE OUT-OF-DATE CHEAT SHEET DRAFTER

1. Ernest Byner
2. Ricky Watters
3. Carl Pickens
4. Antonio Freeman
5. Barry Sanders
6. Jamal Anderson
7. Mark Duper
8. Irving Fryar
9. John Riggins
10. Billy "White Shoes" Johnson

How could this happen? Most often this drafter is simply lazy. And his laziness leads him to a batch of fantasy football magazines that go to print a week after the previous season's Super Bowl. Seeking verification for his purchase, our sheeplike friend eyes the "Sell By" date of early fall, which suggests the information remains current up through his draft.

Evil, evil magazines they are.

And who in the Bush League would value such material? Dr. Goldman, aspiring podiatrist, *nous accussons*.[3]

The manner by which these fantasy rags fall into Adam's hands is quite innocuous, but tragically predictable. At ten a.m., pinching the bridge of his nose, Adam enters the local Target with his fiancée, Ms. Margaret Ming, to buy a gift for her friend's baby shower. But once inside Ming careens off course and starts jibber-jabbering about wicker baskets.

Adam tries to tune her out, but now she's picking her way through

---

3. Our mastery of the French language ceased in the tenth grade, so our confidence that "*nous accussons*" is real French is limited at best. But we think it translates to "we accuse," and that sounds good enough.

a bunch of chintzy "home furnishings." This is his cue to shuffle over to the magazine rack and play some "time off the clock."

At first Adam thumbs through *Newsweek* and feigns outrage at a potential supreme court nominee. Then he turns his attention to the lad magazines: *Maxim, FHM,* and *Loaded.* He scans an interview with scantily clad D-list "actress" Alyssa Milano.

Then, finally, it happens. His eyes fall to the cheaply made covers of fantasy football magazines that are placed next to *Hot Rod* and *Guns & Ammo.* Quickly, he's drawn into their web of deceit. With articles proclaiming the soon to be out-for-the-season David Boston as this year's breakout wide receiver and projections for a monster year from Ricky Williams, the trap is sprung.

On draft day Adam's train wreck is easy to identify. Simply listen for the rapid rustling of papers. This is the sound of the Out-of-Date Cheat Sheet Drafter flailing. Sure, he'll be fine like everyone else in the beginning. But he'll start to unravel by round six.

You'll know it's happening when you hear this conversation:

> **Kwame:** Adam, it's your pick.
> **Adam:** Oh, um, right. [*Shuffle, shuffle*] Okay. Let's see, um, I'll, uh, go with Joe Horn.
> **Kwame:** He was taken. Three rounds ago.
> **Adam:** Oh. [*Rustle, rustle*] Um, okay well, how about— hmm. No, wait, yes. [*Shuffle, rustle*] Okay, how about Dorsey Levens? Is he still available? [*Shuffle*]
> **Kwame:** The Eagles cut him two days ago. Pick someone else.
> **Adam:** [*More rapid rustling*] He was? [*Shuffle, rustle*] I wonder why he's on my cheat sheet?
> **Kwame:** Stop stalling and pick. Pick someone. Anyone.
> **Adam:** [*Now completely flustered*] Fine. [*Shuffle, rustle, shuffle*] I'll take [*Rustle, rustle, rustle*] Ricky Watters.
> **Kwame:** [*Giggles*] Fine. He's all yours. Gentlemen, Ricky Watters is off the board.

It's now curtains for the Out-of-Date Cheat Sheet Drafter. He's been exposed. He's rustled and shuffled his papers, and now he's the owner of the retired Ricky Watters. If only he hadn't been seduced by the *All-Pro, All-Star Fantasy Review.*

THE OVERPREPARED EGGHEAD

The Overprepared Egghead rolls into the conference room ten minutes before the draft, feeling preposterously overconfident. He's outprepared everyone, conducted more research, and done more analysis. There isn't a statistic he doesn't know.

We present to you, Prashun Thind. Or as he states, "Thindy Infante, team manager of the Thindianapolis Colts, present."

He scans the room, slow-blinking at everyone. Then he boots his laptop, and taps rapidly on his keyboard. Up pop a slew of numbers, complicated formulas, and colored charts. None of this really means anything, but it looks impressive to the untrained eye. Some managers steal glances at his monitor.

Thind's pale blue lips curve into a sneer. Soon he begins speaking authoritatively about football insiders like Len Pasquarelli, Chris Mortensen, Ron Jaworski, and Peter King. He won't, however, mention Michael Irvin.

Looking up from his computer, Prash glances at others' cheat sheets and offers unsolicited advice. He nods, saying, "You like Randle El, huh? Not bad, not bad. I really think Pittsburgh is going to get creative with the Z position this year." Other managers are forced to nod back and mutter something about the Z position too. Like they get his point. Like he even gets his point. Like anyone in the Bush League understands anything about the Z position in Pittsburgh.

Finally, having sensed the increased anxiety in the room due to his various bells and whistles, he assumes his Mr. Burns–like repose. Thind punches one more key, numbers flash on the screen, and, with his chin resting on his peaked hands, he slithers, "Excellent."

As the draft begins, Prash starts pecking away at the computer, smiling to himself as if there's a joke that only he's in on. When things start going poorly for other drafters, and their confidence sours, Thind may even let fly with various Bill Walton maxims. "That is just terrrrrriiiibllle," he'll use for starters. Then maybe he'll mix in a "Never mistake activity for achievement" line after another manager spends a long time before whiffing on a pick.

And if he's truly inspired, he may reenact one of the greatest Walton exchanges ever:

> **Bill Walton:** [*Following a tough driving basket by John Stockton*] John Stockton is one of the true marvels, not just of basketball, or in America, but in the history of Western civilization!
> **Tom Hammond:** Wow, that's a pretty strong statement. I guess I don't have a good handle on world history.
> **Bill Walton:** [*Chuckling*] Well, Tom, that's because you didn't go to UCLA.

Walton's commentary, as it applies to the universe as a whole, is simultaneously brilliant and annoying. Kind of like the Overprepared Egghead.

WALTON-ISMS

1. "Tracy McGrady is doing things we've never seen from *anybody*—from *any* planet!"
2. "Mick Jagger is in better shape than far too many NBA players. It's up in the air whether the same can be said of Keith Richards."
3. "Eric Piatkowski makes perhaps the greatest defensive play in Clipper history!"
4. On Larry Johnson's lackluster performance in the NBA finals: "What a pathetic performance by this sad human being. This is a disgrace to the game of basketball and to the NBA. He played like a disgrace tonight. And he deserved it."
5. On his beard: "But you have to understand, my beard is so nasty. I mean, it's the only beard in the history of Western civilization that makes Bob Dylan's beard look good."

Which leads us to the pervasive irony of his situation: All of his preparation ultimately leads to the Egghead's undoing. His laptop is his nerve center, and he's dependent on his technology. So when Thind's second derivation of an algorithm tells him that Hines Ward is a value pick in the second round, he's stuck.

His techno-dependence could lead to other problems. His laptop may freeze, or he may get lost in a flurry of ALT+TABs while monitoring his spreadsheets. With that much data to process there are simply too many things that could go wrong.

Panic sets in. Prash starts punching more violently at his keyboard as his face creeps closer and closer to his screen. But the damage is done. He's lost.

THE FATHER IN MISERY

If you've ever wanted to understand the American Male in Transition—from immature postcollege dope to responsible, protective father—you need only observe the guy who drafts with a child in tow.

The task of identifying the Father in Misery is easy. You don't even need to be in the same room. You can hear him over the speaker-phone. Simply listen for the giggling, cooing, and crying sounds of a baby. If you hear that, you have your man.

Al Lopez is a bundle of contradictions. On the one hand, he's been preparing for his draft for months. On the other, he's a proud father, embracing his role in caring for his young child. Unfortunately for him, these positions are incompatible. The center will not hold.

And how did Lopez find himself in this situation?

The simple answer: his wife, Vanessa.

As with many things in marriage, everything comes down to lever-age. And in Al's case, he has none. Why? Because he's about to spend the next sixteen weeks posted up on his couch, eating pretzels, getting up only to fetch a Coors Light from the fridge.

Yes, for one third of the year he'll be a burden to his wife, useless around the house, and setting a bad example for his kid. Three strikes and he's out. She knows it, his in-laws know it, and even he concedes that he's heading—à la Mark Wahlberg[4] and George Clooney—into choppy waters.

So on the eve of his descent into fantasy football malaise, Vanessa strikes a ninja deathblow. She's going out for a night with the ladies, and leaving him with the kid.

Does Lopez mind? No, honey, of course he doesn't mind. He *can't* mind. Because he's in no position to mind. It's immaterial whether his wife's evening entails sipping sherry by the fire and discussing Oprah's latest book of the month, or going dancing with twenty-year-old boys. Al's fate is sealed. He's drafting with the kid.

---

4. We are referring, of course, to Mr. Wahlberg's strong work in *The Perfect Storm* and not in *Music for the People,* his debut album featuring the inappropriately named Funky Bunch.

And not just any kid—a kid who's on the verge of a meltdown.

This is a devastating early setback, and one from which Al won't recover. He's like a sprinter in the hotly anticipated Olympic 100-meter dash. All his competitors stretch out as they take the blocks. The starter asks for quiet. The gun goes off. The runners explode from the starting line, and about ten meters into the race there's always that one guy who jolts up out of stride, grabs his hammy, grimaces, and fades as the other racers tear down the stretch.

That's the Father in Misery. A bad hamstring pull waiting to happen.

SAD BUT AMUSING SPORTS INJURIES

1. Mary Decker-Slaney getting nicked by Zola Budd in the 1984 Summer Olympics
2. Evel Knievel flying over handlebars inside Wembley Stadium
3. Vinko Bogataj's failed ski jump on ABC's *Wide World of Sports*
4. Scottie Pippen's migraine in game seven against the Detroit Pistons
5. Thomas Hearns smiling, bobbing around the ring on rubber legs before getting knocked out by Sugar Ray Leonard
6. Embarrassing Philadelphia Eagles fans cheering as Michael Irvin lay on the turf with a neck injury
7. Arizona kicker, Bill Grammatica, after hitting a successful field goal, pumping his fist and doing a little leap in the air before landing awkwardly and tearing his ACL

At first everything seems to be going well. Al nails his first few picks and turns to his child with a big grin. Look at proud papa, will you! He's just bagged his first sleeper! El Matador starts doing his salsa half step.

But then the inevitable happens: The kid, largely ignored, rolls his head into the corner of the dining-room table. This leads to a torrent of crying mixed with some whining. Perhaps the child layers in a little more aggressive slapping at his father's cheat sheet, sending pages flying.

Al is now officially miserable.

He puts the child on his shoulder and pats his back. No luck. Then he goes to the swing-the-baby-in-the-air move. The kid isn't impressed. The shrieking builds. Panicking, Al starts bouncing the kid on his knee. But it's too little too late.

During this battle Al receives a double dose of anxiety: Not only is his draft faltering, but he also feels guilty for having such screwed-up priorities. Why can't he be a better father? Why can't he dedicate himself fully to his family? And is fantasy football really so important to him that he'll let his child cry before his very eyes?

The answers to these questions are: We don't know, We don't know, and Yes.

Amid this flurry of deep thoughts and introspection, his sixth-round pick is up. Lopez, having lost track of who's still available, scrambles and takes a tight end, pats his kid on the head, and shuts it down.

His race against time is over.

KIM JONG IL AND THE BITTER DRAFTER

There's always one skunk at the garden party. Some guy who's just *not* happy to be there. On a night that's the equivalent of Christmas Eve for most managers, The Bitter Drafter is expecting coal.

He shuffles into the draft room and takes his seat in silence, his eyes pink and glazed. From time to time he stares at other managers and shakes his head. While most guys engage in the usual predraft hijinks, smack talk, and useless misdirection, he quietly stews.

He looks like Arvydas Sabonis after Rasheed Wallace threw a towel in his face[5] during the Portland Trail Blazers' annual play-off

---

5. Sheed, just before he was traded to Atlanta: "I don't give a (expletive) about no trade rumors. As long as somebody 'CTC,' at the end of the day, I'm with them. For all you that don't know what 'CTC' means, that's 'Cut the Check.'"

meltdown. Sabonis had to be thinking, *I should wipe that dopey birthmark off that howling knucklehead with my big meat hooks, but I'll play it cool.*

Don't think Sabonis forgot about that, though.

This year The Bitter Drafter has it in for The Mick. There could be multiple causes for his agitation. Perhaps it was a bad egg-salad sandwich at lunch, or perhaps he didn't like the rather pointless Koko B. Ware arm motions O'Brien did when he made his picks last year. Honestly, we don't even think that O'Brien *knows* that the Bitter Drafter is after him. Which is even funnier. Because he just might destroy O'Brien's entire season.

If The Bitter Drafter were an international politician, he'd be North Korean maestro Kim Jong Il: someone who openly disregards the principle of mutually assured destruction. Someone who's happy to wear a dopey beige jumpsuit and seventies-style tinted eyewear, spout a few lines of discursive propaganda, and sip brandy as global superpowers collide around him.

DOPEY DICTATORS

1. Saddam Hussein (recently retired, Iraq)—A man who tugged on the tail of the sleeping lion one too many times, and got bit; photographed in his underwear for good measure.
2. Fidel Castro (Cuba)—"The revenues of Cuban state-run companies are used exclusively for the benefit of the people, to whom they belong."
3. Mu'ammar al-Gadhafi (Libya)—Punishes entire towns for "collective guilt." Wears fashionable sunglasses.
4. Mobutu (Zaire)—Wore leopard-skin pillbox hat.
5. L. Ron Hubbard—Led the masses to read *Dianetics*; devotee Tom Cruise ended up bunny-hopping on Oprah's couch.

When it comes to his drafting strategy, all accepted rules of engagement are out the window. The Bitter Drafter derives more satisfaction from wrecking other people's teams than from building his own. Like Kim Jong Il, he uses his irrationality to keep his enemies off balance, all of which leads to him vulturing players of strategic importance from other teams earlier than he should.

Even if The Bitter Drafter hasn't drafted a starting running back yet, that won't stop him from nabbing perennial backups Maurice Morris or Najeh Davenport. The Bitter Drafter aims to spite. His team is finished before the season even begins. But he's hurt your team too, and in the sick mind of The Bitter Drafter, that's a sufficient reason to act.

THE EX–COLLEGE FOOTBALL PLAYER

The Ex–College Football Player enters a draft with a great deal of respect. He greets guys with his deep baritone voice, rubs his closely shorn scalp, and smiles that winning smile, save for the chipped right bicuspid.

He circles the War Room in a Nordstrom's suit that's just a bit too tight across the shoulders, and a shirt collar that's excessively starched. The crispness of his outfit will come into play late in the draft as his stress builds and his neck veins bulge.

Moments before the draft starts, Schlots turns to Goldman and whispers, "Kwame could be a major force this year. He played varsity at Purdue. He has friends in the NFL, and access to inside info."

"Hmmm. Will that really help him?"

"Remains to be seen."

If you have an Ex–College Football Player in your league, you know the drill. He was a backup linebacker at Penn State who used to ball with LaVar Arrington. Or he was the long-snapper at Princeton who used to ball the governor's daughter.

In either case the dude has skills.

Kwame starts the draft with a string of visionary picks. In the third round he takes an emerging wide receiver and says, "My boy James played with this cat in D-II. He says he runs tight routes." Murmurs break out in the draft room. The rest of the Bush League frets over his insider knowledge.

Ultimately, however, Kwame is a sheep in wolf's clothing—dangerous-looking but toothless. Because the Ex–College Football Player evaluates players based on their real skills, as opposed to their far more important fantasy potential. And that's a problem.

The first danger sign is when he adds Cory Schlesinger to his running back stable because "he's a great lead blocker and will be rewarded for his effort with goal-line carries." Then he nabs a backup flanker on the Chiefs because he thinks that "his footwork is sharp and Coach Vermeil will need to get him involved in the passing game." Then he takes Andre Davis because he likes "the work ethic of Virginia Tech players."

PHRASES USED BY THE EX–COLLEGE FOOTBALL PLAYER

1. "I like his burstability."
2. "That guy can do twenty benches at two twenty-five without sweating."
3. "His hands are the softest of any tight end I've seen in the last ten years."
4. "He elevated his stock at the Combine."
5. "My old position coach loves his can-do attitude."

At this point the Ex–College Football Player's knowledge, once a key strength, becomes a weakness. Much as the Empire's fearsome "Scout Walkers (AT-ST)" were felled by the Ewoks' primitive ropes and boulders in the forests of Endor, Kwame now starts lurching forward, mired in his own analysis. By the eighth round he collapses in a heap amid a group of fantasy football Ewoks one third his size, who are dancing around and chanting, "Yubb-yubb!"

This is how it ends for the Ex–College Football Player. Not with a bang but with a trip, a stumble, a thud, and a whimper. The starched shirt is now tight around his neck. His once promising team is now in trouble.

But he remains a good sport. He smiles across the table at the geeky half-pints in his league—guys whom he could snap like Joe Theismann's fibula—who snicker, snicker again, and then crack one joke after another at the big man's expense.

THE TWO-HEADED HYDRA

Every so often you encounter a dual-manager team. The rationale for this pairing is twofold: First, these guys are inherently cheap and are looking for a way to split the league entry fee; and second, they're under the misguided impression that two heads are better than one. But just as a two-headed hydra spends more time snapping at itself than grabbing extra food, so too is this partnership destined for trouble.

The reason it won't work is an absence of leadership. Consider the great military generals throughout history. Did Napoléon have an aide-de-camp he relied upon when rolling across Europe? Did Eisenhower have a peer issuing commands on the beaches of Normandy? Did George W. Bush have a silent partner calling the shots in the march to war in Iraq?

Okay, don't answer that last one. But you get the point. Great leaders make tough decisions unilaterally. And they alone must live with the results.

By way of contrast The Two-Headed Hydra believes in consensus-driven management. They've coordinated their first few picks, and may even exchange an audible high five when their guy falls to them at the end of the second round. But even then, fissures begin to show.

> **Guy #1:** Booyah! Daunte Culpepper fell to us.
> **Guy #2:** Solid scouting, partner.
> **Guy #1:** Booyah!
> **Guy #2:** Dude, stop yelling "Booyah!" You're hurting my ears.

And so it begins. They're already snapping at each other. Now it's just a matter of time before they disagree on a pick, start debating useless stats, and their system breaks down completely.

If they're calling in to the draft, you might hear muffled phone conversations, the ruffling of papers, one insisting that they "stick with the system" and the other arguing that they "follow our gut."

This wasn't the plan. They took a tight end early, and missed out on a slew of running backs. Now they can't agree on anything.

When Lopez says, "Hustle up, you're on the clock," they tell him to take it easy. They stall. They hem. They haw.

And then, when everyone tells them to pick—that they have to pick, *now*—they settle on the dreaded "middle option." In the sixth round they take Keyshawn Johnson, a player neither of them could possibly want, which will only lead to more Hydra-snapping for the rest of the draft.

THE GUY WHO LOVES ROOKIES

There's something odd about the Guy Who Loves Rookies. Coaches don't like rookies. Teammates don't like rookies. Rookies often don't even like rookies. So what does that say about the manager who only drafts young punks for his fantasy football team?

We point to the tao of *Dazed and Confused* for a potential answer. In this film Matthew McConaughey's character says wistfully, "That's what I love about these high school girls, man. I get older, they stay the same age."

The Guy Who Loves Rookies is obsessed with youth—infatuated with nubile prodigies to near perversion. Rookies offer promise, upside, and excitement.

"I love fresh meat," Schlots announces to no one in particular. He then reinforces his declaration by stating, "Give me young legs, give me young knees."

His obsession for young talent began during his undergrad years. Hours logged watching ESPN's *College GameDay* planted the seed. Kirk Herbstreit shimmered on camera, Lee Corso donned the local college hat and foam finger, and our man got all misty-eyed.

Back then the hot college player du jour was running through Rutgers's turnstile defensive line, and Keith Jackson let fly with a half-dozen "Whoa Nellies!" Finally this rookie was cemented in Schlots's mind when, at the NFL draft, Mel Kiper Jr. uttered some nonsense about how he "grades out" to be the greatest at his position in the last decade. Or, possibly, ever.

Then John Clayton rolled his eyes, Chris Berman gave him a nickname, and the player slow-limped up to the stage in some ill-fitting six-piece suit equipped with a dangling timepiece. Perhaps he even had a top hat or a cane. And just like that the manager was locked in—that was his guy. He fell in love right there with the rookie's pimpiness.

It's true that the Guy Who Loves Rookies *can* put together a decent team every three or four years. Just look at Schlots, who managed to secure his first championship ring behind the video-game-like highlight reel that was Clinton Portis during his first NFL campaign.

And yes, few things are more exciting than rolling the dice on a highly touted rookie and coming up with double sixes. Taking Edgerrin James in 1999 and seeing him run roughshod over the NFL, silver teeth gleaming after one of his 17 TDs, was better than winning big in Vegas, better than a lap dance at Scores, better even than taking a savvy veteran who'd posted equally gaudy numbers the year before.

But for every Edge there are six Ron Daynes. For every Randy

Moss there are a half-dozen Charles Rogers. These guys will cripple most fantasy teams. That doesn't stop the Guy Who Loves Rookies from taking them, though. The thrill of the hunt is too strong, the scent of fresh meat too intoxicating, and the allure of the next big thing too overwhelming.

A ROOKIE MIGHT PAN OUT IF . . .

1. He *isn't* a quarterback. Peyton Manning, Michael Vick, and Donovan McNabb all had miserable rookie campaigns.
2. He *is* a running back. Over the last seven years at least one rookie has finished in the top ten among running backs for fantasy scoring. (That being said, according to ESPN, running backs drafted in the NFL's first round over the last ten years have averaged a measly 654 rushing yards and 4 touchdowns.)
3. He isn't taken in the first five rounds. Chances are, fresh meat fetishists will overvalue young players to the point of leaving better options on the table.

So he assembles his team full of promise, pep, and optimism. His squad is exciting—on paper, at least. But it will crumble by week two when Coach Shanahan decides that his rookie running back can't block. Or Eli Manning coughs up three picks during his first start.

And that is that.

THE DEATH MAIDEN

Susan B. Anthony, she of the useless one-dollar coin and champion of women's suffrage, once said, "It is a downright mockery to talk to women of their enjoyment of the blessings of liberty while they are denied the use of the only means of securing them provided by this Democratic-Republican government—the ballot."

We're not sure what any of that really means, or what liberty has to do with fantasy football. But perhaps it speaks to the need, nay right, of women to participate equally with men in any activity. To prohibit women from doing so would mock the very freedoms that soldiers have given their lives to defend.

Yesteryear's ballot box is today's fantasy football league.

Or something like that.

The emergence of women in fantasy football, however, will never be smooth. The seeds of hostility between the sexes actually predate the advent of fantasy football. It started, we surmise, in the realm of Dungeons & Dragons—when men were boys, boys were dorks, and girls found them irritating.

This phenomenon was captured perfectly in the following scene from *Wet Hot American Summer*:

> **Caped Boy:** Excuse me, ladies. You may remember me as the guy who came to dinner a few weeks ago with underwear on my head. . . . And as you may have heard, I am recently a crowned class-B dungeon master. So if any of you would like to play D&D today, please speak now or forever hold your peace.
> [*He chuckles, and there is an awkward silence at the table.*]
> Anyone? Alexa! Maybe you would like to join in? We do need a druid, and you have definitely cast a level-5 charm spell on me.
> **Alexa:** In your dreams, douche bag!
> **Caped Boy:** Douche bags are hygienic products; I take that as a compliment. Thank you.

Men haven't forgotten that adolescent scorn. Today when a woman enters the male-dominated fantasy football arena, there's always friction because men are afraid of being trumped by women in anything sports-related.

Which is why female managers are the ultimate stealth-bombers. They show up at the draft, looking skittish and acting clueless. But by flying beneath the radar and not overthinking everything, they're able to assemble lethal teams with simple commonsense picks.

At the start of the draft Thind eyes The Death Maiden and mutters, "She may be able to cook up a mean meat loaf, but what does she know about the Chargers' receiving corps?"

Big mistake. In a cunning bit of fantasy football jujitsu, women use to their advantage their inexperience, their lack of football knowledge, and their inability to chew kielbasa and grapes at the same time. They flip it.

While men run regression models gauging the breakout likelihood of third-year wide receivers, women ponder bigger questions, such as: Who has the nicer uniforms? What charities does he support? And which quarterback has prettier eyes?

The myopic guy scoffs at these questions, but the savvy guy fears them. Because he knows that whenever there's a woman in the league, you're all but guaranteed to look up in week five and see her near the top of the standings, cheering for a running back like Tiki Barber, because "he seems so articulate and like such a nice guy. Plus he's a twin—that's cute."

These are the same women who always seem to run the table in the March Madness tourney brackets. They couldn't tell you the difference between La Salle University and the University of Louisville, but they pick fifteen of the sweet-sixteen teams. No one knows precisely how they do it, they just do.

THE REST OF THE RIFFRAFF

In the interest of time we've excluded full descriptions of other draft archetypes. But below you'll find our honorable mentions.

1. **The Guy Who Takes His Defense and Kicker Too Early**
2. **The Guy Who Drafts on a Bad Cell Phone**
3. **The Hometown Drafter:** The Pats fan who grabs David Givens, Kevin Faulk, and Daniel Graham
4. **The Guy Who Elongates Player Names:** In announcing his picks, he chooses to say, "Clintonius Portis," "Frederick Taylor," "Chadwick Johnson," "Edward Kennison," "Torrence Holt," and "Touraj Houshmandzadeh."
5. **The Drunk Drafter**
6. **The Guy Who Favors Players from His Alma Mater**
7. **The Guy Who Searches for Position Loopholes:** Nabs Jimmy Kleinsasser as a fullback/tight end/h-back
8. **The Guy Who Drafts Exceptional Special Teamers (aka "The Dante Hall Drafter")**
9. **The Guy Who Tries to Retract His Pick:** Makes his pick, waits two or three picks, then asks if anyone minds if he cycles a different player in
10. **The Guy Who Drafts Players Based on the Hiring of a New Offensive Line Coach**

4

<< SCENES FROM >> THE DRAFT

O'Brien, Thind, The Bitter Drafter, Kwame, and Goldman enter the War Room. O'Brien does two laps around the conference table and then takes a seat. With big smiles plastered across their faces, the guys exchange welcomes: "What's up, fellas?" "Good to see you!" "I can't believe it's been a year already."

Everyone participates in these pleasantries . . . except for The Bitter Drafter, who scowls, opens his briefcase, and places his cheat sheets in front of him.

Schlots then shows up with a black garbage bag slung over his shoulder. "The Champ is here," he says. The room remains silent. "The Champ is prepared to defend his title." More silence.

Schlots reaches into his bag and pulls out a crumpled fantasy magazine, a horned Viking helmet (which he promptly puts on), and the Bush League trophy, aka the Schmuck Cup. All eyes fall on the copper-tinted trophy that was purchased five years before in a hardware store for $19.99.

7:49 P.M.

Thind takes out his computer and starts hammering away. Then he opens his briefcase and retrieves a package wrapped in newspaper. He holds it in the palm of his hand, then slides it down the table to O'Brien.

"What is it?"

"Just open it."

"No."

"C'mon. You know you want to."

O'Brien finally unfolds the paper.

He finds a package of Van de Kamp's fish sticks.

"What the hell?"

"It's a Sicilian message," Thind says. "It means, Tonight McFish sleeps with the fishes." Thind giggles. O'Brien curses silently. The other managers shake their heads and return to their cheat sheets.

7:59 P.M.

Al Lopez patches into the conference call, the faint squealing of a baby in the background. Three seconds later The Two-Headed Hydra beeps in, but one of the two managers can't hear anything. "What? Hello? What's happening? Has the draft started yet?"

8:00 P.M.

Thind and Goldman are shadowboxing—throwing jabs, uppercuts, and making weird snorting sounds. Schlots is shaking the Schmuck Cup over his head, hopping from foot to foot. Kwame is patting his big mitts together and saying, "It's on, gentlemen. It's on." Anticipation in the War Room is at an all-time high. There's frenetic laughter and shouting and general jibber-jabber, until . . .

8:01 P.M.

"Gentlemen," Kwame says, and the room falls into complete silence. "We're ready to begin this year's Bush League Fantasy Football Draft. Adam Goldman has the first pick. Team Goyim, you . . . are . . . on the clock." There's nervous laughter and heavy breathing. The world seems to be moving in slow motion. A voice on the conference call says, "Here it comes . . ."

8:02 P.M.

"Team Goyim selects . . ." Even though he's had this decision made for weeks, Goldman can't help but think it over one last time. "Team Goyim selects . . . hold on a sec."

Schlots mutters, "Let's go, let's go."

"Team Goyim selects . . . from Waco, Texas . . . LaDainian Tomlinson."

"There goes LT2," says Thind. The other managers nod before scratching Tomlinson off their cheat sheets. O'Brien, who occupies the lowly eleventh spot, adds, "I guess he won't be there for me."

8:06 P.M.

The inevitable has happened: Six straight running backs taken. They're going down faster than bad guys in a Dirty Harry movie. Now the managers at the bottom of the draft are sweating, wondering if they'll have to settle for a wide receiver or worse . . . a quarterback.

8:09 P.M.

With nine running backs gone, The Mick is now on the clock. And, as Schlots predicted, he is indeed "up around the bend."

O'Brien concentrates on his cheat sheet and scowls. Schlots starts chanting, "Reach! Reach! Reach!"

"Could you be quiet, please? I'm trying to concentrate."

Other Bush League managers pound the table. "Reach! Reach! Reach!"

For five weeks The Mick has been preparing for this pick. But now that he's up, he's hit by a wave of ambivalence. "Uh, give me a second, guys."

Lopez says, "Just do it—walk the plank."

"I'm asking again, please be quiet. Show some courtesy."

"Get 'er done, O'Brien."

"Uh, okay. I'm ready—no, no I'm not."

"O'Brien," Kwame says, "your time is up."

"Okay, okay. I'm going to take . . ."

"Reach! Reach! Reach!"

Swallowing hard, The Mick selects . . . a wide receiver.

"Ouch."

Seconds later O'Brien concludes that his draft is doomed. The last thing in the world that he wanted to do was take a wide receiver in the first round—now he has no chance of locking up two viable starting running backs.

Some men see the glass as half-full, some men see it as half-empty, and some men—men like O'Brien—chuck the glass against the wall. Which is exactly what he does. He takes his beer mug and he slams it against a very white wall in a very expensive conference room inside the offices of a very luxurious investment bank.

"Well, that was smart," Thind says. "Real smart."

O'Brien just ignores him. "Christ! Nine backs gone. *Gone.*" He picks up his cheat sheet and draws an X straight through the middle. He's officially unhinged.

"Temper, temper," says The Bitter Drafter.

BRUTAL DRAFT SPOTS

Seventh Pick: In running-back-heavy leagues this is the first wobbly-knee spot. You're either taking a flyer on a shaky running back or breaking with popular wisdom and reaching for a wide receiver.

Eleventh Pick: Up around the bend indeed. Not much good can come of this position, especially since you have a Death Valley–like wait until the third round.

Twelfth Pick: No one we know has ever done well with this spot. Ever. Worse, this spot always seems to go to a newbie who flails early.

8:14 P.M.

In back-to-back picks (the last pick of the first round and the first pick of the second round) The Two-Headed Hydra takes two quarterbacks, causing a wave of groans, adjusted Excel models, and cheat sheet edits.

"Those are great picks," Thind says. "In the tenth and eleventh rounds."

And so it goes—the first official loose cannon picks have thrown the Bush League into chaos. Managers who don't make the expected value-based pick at their position can cause great anxiety for everyone in the league. They're the blackjack players in Vegas who hit on fourteen with the dealer showing a six—no one behind them feels like he's getting the right card.

8:15 P.M.

A somewhat relieved O'Brien takes a second-year running back that he'd expected to be off the board. He can't believe his good luck.

The rest of the league potshots The Two-Headed Hydra.

"Hydra, you are the Cleveland Browns of the Bush League."

"Hydra: two managers, two draft picks . . . two terrible decisions."

"Hydra, how can it go this bad this early?"

O'Brien, meanwhile, calls his boy the "steal of the draft." Then he makes a fist and shakes it. In mere minutes O'Brien has gone from a fallen man to a gloating SOB.

Schlots says, "It's better to be lucky than good."

"I'm not lucky," responds O'Brien.

"You're not good," says Schlots.

O'Brien glares at Schlots.

Schlots looks down and makes random notations on his cheat sheet. He then highlights his notations.

8:18 P.M.

At the end of the second round Goldman says, "I'm going to regret this pick, right?"

"Probably," Thind says. "We don't know. Just pick."

"I'm going to regret this, I know it."

He is met with a collective shrug.

Goldman does not have an easy decision. The obvious selections are gone. He can take a running back with questions, one of ten decent wide receivers, all of whom will have similar stats, or a quarterback.

"I can't take this guy . . . can't take this guy . . . No, fuck it, I'm taking him. Team Goyim selects . . ."

Thind is laughing uncomfortably.

"Team Goyim selects . . . Tiki Barber."

"Yep," Thind says, "you'll regret that."[6]

8:25 P.M.

Al Lopez makes his first shushing sound to his son. A rattle drops in the background.

---

6. Tiki Barber is one of those rare fantasy studs who, despite having several solid seasons, is not desired by Bush League managers. No one can explain why. Perhaps it's his name.

8:37 P.M.

In the fourth round, for reasons that are clear only to the gods of fantasy football, there's a run on tight ends. Four go down in six picks. Then everyone comes to their senses and the draft continues.

PREDICTABLE RUNS

Stud running backs (01.01–01.12). If ten running backs don't go in the first twelve picks, your league is full of guppies.

Wide receivers (02.06–03.10). Some managers go RB-WR-RB. Others go RB-RB-WR. Either way, most elite wide receivers are taken by the end of the third round.

Tight ends (03.08–04.12). When Tony Gonzalez goes, so go the three other popular tight ends with unjustified hype. We can't say that this makes much sense.

Backup running backs (07.01–08.12). A rather mean-spirited game of chicken, as managers try to poach promising second-string RBs.

Kickers and defenses (15.01–16.12). Exhaustion and a need to meet roster specs lead to the most uninspired run of the night.

8:41 P.M.

The Two-Headed Hydra asks, "What round are we in?"
The Bitter Drafter answers, "What round do you think we're in?"
A long pause, and then The Hydra replies, "An early round?"

"Kwame, do we have their league fees?"

Kwame says yes.

"Very well, Hydra, you're entirely correct: We're in an early round."

8:48 P.M.

Kwame interrupts the draft to make the following announcement: "Folks, I've been informed that the following trade has occurred. Team Goyim and The Death Maiden have swapped picks in the third, fourth, and sixth rounds. Please be advised." A hurricane of conversation commences as managers attempt to assess the trade.

"Um, excuse me," Thind says. "Who has Jeremy Shockey?"

"I have Shockey," The Hydra says.

"You sure about that, Hydra?"

"Pretty sure. Let me double-check. Yep!"

"Wait a minute, so who moved whom where?"

"I'll send you an update," The Death Maiden says. "After the draft."

"Wait," Thind says, "can she do that?"

"She can do that," Kwame says definitively.

"Nice job there, Death Maiden," Schlots says.

"Thanks."

"What about me?" Goldman asks.

"We'll talk later, Goldman."

8:49 P.M.

The Mick claims that the recently approved trade is absolutely, 100 percent unfair. A complete travesty. An utter abomination. Team Goyim *must* have taken advantage of The Death Maiden.

He demands that Kwame veto the trade, but Kwame ignores him.

The Death Maiden maintains a serene gaze. She clearly knows

more than she's letting on. Goldman, however, appears considerably less confident. He's tilting his head back, staring at the ceiling, counting draft spots on his fingers.

8:54 P.M.

In the sixth and seventh rounds, after The Bitter Drafter takes two backup running backs, O'Brien tells him, "Bitter Drafter, you realize that we don't have a flex position in this league; you can't start those guys at wide receiver."

The Bitter Drafter glares at O'Brien and holds his thumb up.

"What? What are you doing?" asks O'Brien.

The Bitter Drafter then turns his thumb down.

"That would appear to be rather bad news for you," Thind chips in.

9:03 P.M.

The Hydra asks, "What round are we in?" Schlots scratches his armpits, then asks to "borrow" Goldman's fantasy football magazines. Goldman refuses his request.

"That's rather Jew-ey of you," Schlots says.

Thind asks other managers what their take on Marcus Pollard is this year, then smiles cryptically. Psychological warfare abounds.

9:14 P.M.

A child is wailing in the background. Through a muffled phone Al Lopez is heard saying, *"Precioso, papa está preocupado, oh-kay?"*

Thind fires back with a rather poor Tony Montana impersonation: "Amigo, the only thing in this world that gives orders is balls. Balls. You got that?"

9:23 P.M.

Over the span of two rounds The Bitter Drafter snags both of The Mick's backup running backs. There will be no "handcuffing" of picks for O'Brien tonight.

Kwame says, "I guess that's what the whole thumbs-down thing meant."

The Bitter Drafter nods to himself.

The Mick vows to kill the women and children of those who have betrayed him. Goldman calls O'Brien "Palestinian-esque."

9:32 P.M.

Thind Uzi-taps the arrow keys on his laptop before making his pick. "Go with your gut," Schlots says. "That thing can't make all your picks for you, can it?"

Thind presses his fingers together and tells him to relax, just relax—everything's going *exactly* according to plan.

9:35 P.M.

O'Brien looks at Schlots and says, "Guess what The Mick has cookin' for you?" Schlots shrugs. The Mick nabs Schlots's backup quarterback. "How do you like them apples?"

Schlots shrugs again. "I don't know," he says. "I guess that's what you need to do *up around the bend.*"

The Mick is furious, trembling.

9:45 P.M.

The Hydra asks, "What round are we in?" Then, after much confusion, they take their second straight defense. Thind says, "Ah, *now* I understand.

You're employing the 'guppy strategy'—pairing an anemic offense with very strong defenses, eh?" The Hydra doesn't respond. "Watch out, these guys will be zone blitzing this fall." Thind gets nothing. "They're the Baltimore Ravens of the Bush League." Silence. "They're the—"

"Enough, Prashun," Kwame says. "Enough."

ANATOMY OF A GUPPY DRAFT

Rounds 1 and 2: Good QB, Reach QB
Round 3: Oft-injured, high-flying RB
Round 4: Jeremy Shockey
Round 5: Antowain Smith
Rounds 6–9: Chiefs and Browns wide receivers
Rounds 10–11: Back-to-back defenses
Rounds 12–13: David Boston and, inexplicably, a third QB
Rounds 14–18: Repeated calls for players already taken, followed by riffraff

9:47 P.M.

The Death Maiden takes Tom Brady, her starting quarterback, in the eighth round. She's pretty much getting the same value quarterback here as other quarterbacks taken three rounds earlier. Suddenly the rest of the Bush League is examining her team.

"Not bad," O'Brien says.

"Respectable," Thind adds.

"Could be trouble," Kwame says.

9:52 P.M.

Goldman announces that if people don't hurry up, he's going to have to leave early. This leads to a round of "Your fiancée has you whipped" taunts.

"Seriously, guys," Kwame says. "We need to limit our picks to a minute each, or we'll be here all night." Other managers grumble. But the draft continues at a Ron Dayne snail-like pace.

9:55 P.M.

The Mick approaches The Bitter Drafter and says, "Sorry about what happened earlier. I hope that everything's cool."

"What's done is done," The Bitter Drafter says.

The Mick doesn't entirely understand this response. "So we're cool?"

"We are what we are."

"Right. Anyway, I was hoping that I could show you something."

The Bitter Drafter doesn't respond.

The Mick sits down next to him and diagrams a trade on graph paper. There are arrows and triangles drawn, and a big looping spiral. The Mick is sitting very close to The Bitter Drafter, perhaps too close. The Bitter Drafter listens for a while, and then makes a "shoo fly" motion with his left hand. "What?" The Mick asks. Again The Bitter Drafter makes the same "shoo fly" hand gesture. "What are you saying?"

"Scamper. I'm telling you to scamper."

10:40 P.M.

The Hydra's on the clock in the thirteenth round.

"We'll go with Elam."

"Taken."

"Okay then, Morten Andersen."

"Old, gone."

A silence envelops the War Room. O'Brien is pacing. "Goddamnit," he says. "Pick, Hydra. Just pick."

"Uh . . . Mare?"

"Gentlemen," Kwame says, "Olindo Mare is off the board."

Schlots says, "From the University of Notre Dame, a former member of the Fighting Irish and now a member of The Fat Minnesota Guys . . . Julius Jones . . . Jones."

Kwame tells him that he hates it when he does that.

"When I do what?"

"When you state the guy's name twice, for one thing—"

"Oh? That bothers you?"

"And also when you tell everyone that a guy's from Notre Dame. We know where Julius Jones went to school, all right?"

"Listen," Schlots says, hands spread wide, "I'm a Domer, I can't help but—"

"Fuck the Dome," Kwame says.

Schlots chews on his lower lip. "Did you just say, 'Fuck the Dome'?"

"Yeah," Kwame says. "Fuck the Dome, and fuck the Grotto, and fuck Lou Holtz and fuck the Gipper."

11:05 P.M.

In the sixteenth round Prash takes Ricky Williams.

Goldman asks, "Will the Thindianapolis Colts also be taking D. B. Cooper?"

"I like his option value," Thind purrs.

"What? What are you talking about?"

"I like Ricky Williams's optionality."

11:15 P.M.

In the final round a phone clicks off, then comes back on, and then there's a buzzing sound.

"Al?" Kwame asks.

"I'm here."

"Hydra? . . . Hydra? . . . Hello, Hydra?" Kwame says. "Ladies and gentlemen, Hydra has left the building." Thind makes a final scroll through his Excel spreadsheet, ball-hawking for any undrafted gems.

12:30 A.M.

The draft concludes. Schlots reclines in his chair, a smile on his face. "This has been the greatest three hours of the year."

El Matador concurs, "Thanks, boys. It's been fun."

Thind announces that, on behalf of the Bush League, he'd like to thank Kwame for running such a smooth draft. Kwame nods, presses the off button of the speakerphone, and says, "Welcome to the Terror Dome."

<< POSTDRAFT >> REACTIONS

IF FANTASY FOOTBALL IS LIKE HAVING A RELATIONSHIP,
then your draft is the first date. It can set the tone for a wonderful
journey full of deep spiritual commitment. But if things go poorly,
you're out a hundred and fifty bucks, and unlikely to score.

Perceptions matter. Your first evening with your new team says a lot
about your self-confidence. How did you draft? Is your running back
stable full? Are your receivers explosive? And who's your kicker?

UNDERRATED MUPPETS

1. Snufalufagus—solid, up-the-middle rapport with Big Bird
2. Zoot—calming influence on Animal
3. Salacious Crumb—Jabba the Hut's pet
4. Rizzo and the rest of the Rat Pack
5. Camilla the Chicken—Gonzo's lover

Thomas Paine once said, "I love the man that can smile in trouble,
that can gather strength from distress, and grow brave by reflection."

So, were you Guy Smiley[7] confidently explaining multiplication tables, or Beaker after another Dr. Bunsen Honeydew experiment gone awry?

These questions—Muppet-based or otherwise—matter. How you drafted says a lot about you. And in turn, your fellow managers' reactions to the draft reveal what they think of themselves.

THE MATERIAL CONSUMER REACTION

Every year at least one Bush League manager leaves the War Room saying, "I love it when a plan comes together." Cracking his knuckles, he adds, "It was all so easy—I was in the zone."

And what inspires this confidence?

Some guys are drawn to players-of-the-moment. Driven by an alchemy of fantasy magazines, Internet experts, and fellow league members, they grab a *hot* "stud" running back (Shaun Alexander), a *hot* second running back ready to explode in a new system (Duce Staley), a *brand name* "stud" wide receiver (Chad Johnson), a *hot* wide receiver coming off a breakout year (Santana Moss), and a *brand name* "winning" quarterback (Tom Brady). Sprinkle in a sleeper like DeShaun Foster, and this manager is good to go.

Most savvy drafters will recognize these names as "legitimate up-and-comers," which will only strengthen this manager's feelings about his team. Going with a trendy receiver who's never had more than 1,000 yards is far more important to him than taking someone like Marvin Harrison, a proven—albeit boring—workhorse.

Because the Material Consumer needs flashy options at each position.

Thind has assembled a team in this vein, and so has The Mick, who, after stumbling badly in the first round, notes, "I can't believe that so much talent fell to me. I mean, look at all my babies, dropping into Daddy's lap."

And what do The Mick and Thind have in common, besides unjustifiable self-confidence? Well, for one thing they're semiwealthy

7. Who may or may not have been the same Muppet as Don Music, but that's immaterial.

single guys in a big city. They like to have good shit. The fastest cars. The newest gizmos. The trendiest clothes. The slickest apartments.

"Let me lock in a plasma HDTV," the single guy says to himself, "so that I can get the full effect of *Bullitt* on DVD. Let me get my Armani slacks tailored. Let me buy a BlackBerry—even if the only e-mails I get are fantasy football trade offers."

OTHER MATERIAL CONSUMER PURCHASES

1. Vintage Minneapolis Lakers jersey
2. Granite countertops
3. Framed copy of "Kind of Blue"
4. Inordinately complicated wine-bottle opener
5. BMW Roadster

He enjoys ostentatious displays of wealth, and this mentality shapes his perception of his team. His reaction to the draft is pure chest-thumping. O'Brien crows, "With proven brand names like these, I'm minted!"

Thind kicks back, hands behind his head, and stares smugly. He's got his own brand-name team—a team full of players that everyone recognizes. He can talk to friends outside the Bush League, describe his team, and get the affirming "nice draft" head-nod. All that's left is to mount his prized plasma forty-eight-incher, order the NFL Sunday Ticket, and watch the show unfold.

THE CHICKEN LITTLE REACTION

The mirror opposite of the Material Consumer, the Chicken Little *hates* his team. Before the season has even begun, he's ready to take a knee. "I'm shutting it down," he says to no one in particular.

Adam Goldman, our resident Chicken Little, has never drafted a team that he's liked. Just now he's scanning his cheat sheet, wondering where it all went wrong.

"I'm finished," he says. "I'm toast."

"What's wrong?" Schlots asks. "You had a solid draft."

Goldman runs down his roster. "Dude, I *hate* Tiki Barber."

"He's a top-ten performer."

"I don't care. He's . . . frickin' . . . Tiki."

"Then why did you draft him?"

Goldman stares off into the middle distance. "I don't know, man . . . I just don't know."

Truth be told, Goldman's team isn't really that bad. He made respectable picks in every round, and that left him with a cadre of reasonable but unexciting players: Drew Bledsoe, Isaac Bruce, Laveranues Coles, and Tiki. Not good, but also not terrible. Goldman simply has buyer's remorse.

Unlike Goldman, some Chicken Littles have legitimate reasons for concern. They got caught at the end of a position run, they misjudged a training-camp battle, or they made the critical mistake of taking a backup quarterback before securing a starting running back. These can all be mortal wounds, dooming a fledgling fantasy squad.

Goldman doesn't have this problem, but he might as well. Because he does not believe in his team. No matter how hard he squints, none of the pieces fit. His season is over before it ever began.

THE FAITH-BASED REACTION

On his Web site, famed 700 Club founder and spiritual leader Pat Robertson writes, *"The first secret is to have faith in God—to understand that in God all things are possible."*[8]

Robertson's spiritual counterpart, Jerry Falwell, adds, "If you're not a born-again Christian, you're a failure as a human being." That sounds like

---

8. Mr. Robertson also generously offers believers his famous "Age-Defying Protein Pancakes." For more information, check out: http://www.700club.com/communitypublic/pancakes.asp.

bad news for many of us. So we suppose there are limits to everything.

The Faith-Based Reaction, as it pertains to fantasy football, is to have religious zeal for your team—even if no one else in the league thinks you'll win more than three games all season.

INTRADIVISIONAL RIVALRIES IN EVANGELICAL CHRISTIANITY

1. Jim Bakker pays $265,000 to Jessica Hahn to keep sexual affair a secret. Bakker is later convicted for fraud, tax evasion, and racketeering.
2. Jerry Falwell calls Bakker the "greatest scab and cancer on the face of Christianity in two thousand years of church history." Falwell later states that homosexuals will "be utterly annihilated and there will be celebration in heaven."
3. Jimmy Swaggart calls Bakker "a cancer on the body of Christ" for his infidelities. Later claims rival evangelist Marvin Gorman had an affair.
4. Gorman, seeking revenge, flattens Swaggart's tires, gets cameras, and takes pictures of Swaggart exiting a Baton Rouge hotel with a prostitute.
5. After getting caught speeding with another prostitute, Swaggart claims that he's "made right with God."

John Schlotterbeck is big on "the whole belief-system thang." He has absolutely no doubts about any player that he drafts. He's convinced, for example, that his quarterback, Tommy Maddox, is bound for a huge year: This defies all reason and statistical evidence, but no one can talk him out of this.

"Schlots, you look a little shaky at quarterback," Lopez says.

"No, not at all. I'm fine with Maddox."

"C'mon, the guy's had more concussions than Steve Young."

"He's breezed through preseason."

"Schlots, seriously, be reasonable—the guy has had seven or eight good games. Tops. You can't pin your entire season on him."

"I have faith. I believe in my man."

So it goes with the faith-based drafter. He believes. That's what he does. He believes in his quarterback, and he believes in his stable of backup running backs. In his mind they're all due to emerge as starters; it's only a matter of time. Nick Goings may be a third-string scrub for the Carolina Panthers, but for Schlots he's just two pulled hammies away from stud status.

Don't burden yourself with past performance or so-called stats. Where Schlots comes from, that's all just "fuzzy math" that Northeastern academics (read: Jews) obsess over.[9]

Schlots is fired up about his team and undaunted by any criticism. "The Fat Minnesota Guys are primed for *another* championship run. We have faith in all of our players at every position. And faith will lead us to glory."

THE BARKLEY POST-UP REACTION

During his prime, Charles Barkley got the ball in the post, dribbled it fifteen times, and ass-backed his way into the paint. Sir Charles was never going to cross over an opponent or shoot a soft runner in the lane. He just banged away.

In fantasy football, the Barkley Post-Up manager plays it safe during the draft. He more or less avoids flashiness. He could have burned a high draft pick on Ricky Williams, only to find that Ricky had opted for retirement, growing a patchy beard and rolling spliffs on the Australian seashore.

That could have happened. But it didn't.

---

9. As far as Catholics go, Schlots isn't particularly anti-Semitic. He's just puzzled by why the Jews "run banks and movie companies, and yell all the time about mishmash."

BARKLEY-ISMS

1. "I heard Tonya Harding is calling herself the Charles Barkley of figure skating. I was going to sue her for defamation of character, but then I realized I have no character."
2. On facing Cuba in the '92 Olympics: "What do I know about Cuba? The country is run by a scruffy-looking guy who smokes cigars—that's all I know."
3. "I know why his name is DMX. Because his real name is Earl. Imagine if his name was Earl the Rapper."
4. "Every time I think about changing a diaper, I run a little bit harder and a little bit faster to make sure I can afford a nanny until my daughter's old enough to take care of that herself."

The post-up manager is an acolyte of the "stud running back" theory. Get two horses that you can rely on each week, play the percentages, and everything will be fine. It may not be the sexiest or most exciting strategy. But it gets the job done.

The manager who uses the Barkley Post-Up values stability. He has other, more important priorities in his life and simply wants to put together a solid team. He's not easily impressed by flash-in-the-pan players, opting instead for proven veterans.

These days, Al Lopez personifies the Post-Up Reaction. He's got his baby boy, who though distracting during the draft is still *his* boy. And he has his wife, Vanessa, who loves him, and makes him dinner. That's a family. And that, he reassures himself, is the big picture.

As the dust settles on the draft, Lopez stands over his desk and studies his team. He basks in the comfort of his two stud running backs. There will be no need to shuttle players in and out of his lineup. No need to swing a slew of high-octane trades. No reason to monitor the free-agent list for the hot available player of the week.

That sort of activity is for the more crazed guys of the league.

That's not Lopez's style anymore. His son, baby Oscar, changed all that.

It's time to post-up. Let the game come to him.

This *may* not be his year. He may not win it all. But he'll contend for the title. And that's good enough. That's how his team is constructed. Slow and steady, churning forward, locking in opportunities for wins.

Lopez flips on his stereo and cues up the Bee Gees' "How Deep Is Your Love." He does a restrained "El Matador Shuffle" as baby Oscar dangles from his arm.

"I got things under control, Oscar," Al says. "Give papa a hug."

THE "SPIN STOPS HERE" REACTION

Fantasy football is a zero sum game. Instill doubt in an opponent, and you feel emboldened. Find weaknesses in other teams, and you'll feel stronger.

Any guy worth his salt knows how to methodically scan another manager's lineup for faults. This includes offering vapor analysis of team structure, misleading player projections, and, in almost every instance, outright false information on a given player's backups.

All points must be couched in faux-objective terms. The trick is to seem calm and measured while asserting unsubstantiated opinion.

You must spin without seeming like you're spinning.

"I hear Priest Holmes has a hitch in his hip," O'Brien says to Kwame.

"O'Brien, I don't have time for your nonsense."

"I swear to God. I heard a doctor discussing it last night. He has a lower-ligament hip hitch." He whistles. "'Hitchitis' is the medical term, I believe."

"Name the show and name the doctor."

"Errr, I have that info somewhere. . . ." O'Brien abandons that line of reasoning and goes to Plan B. "Well, Larry Johnson is looking tight—I was also going to mention that. He'll probably steal a hundred touches. Easy."

"O'Brien, leave me alone."

Once a conversation like this starts, other managers pile on. They're like ants swarming over a leftover doughnut. Thind adds, "Something else you might want to think about is the deep ball." Thind's tone is conciliatory. "Sal Paolantonio says that Trent Green will be chucking the rock all year. You heard that bit, right?"

"Get serious. It's Priest. I'm all set."

"All indications are that Eddie Kennison will be flying."

"Yup," O'Brien says. "Heard that too."

Thind and O'Brien high-five each other. Kwame isn't paying attention to them, but the damage has been done. This sort of verbal warfare has strategic value. And also, it's just fun to spin.

Consider Bill O'Reilly.

While he rants and raves and hoots and hollers about a so-called No Spin Zone, his genius is that he does just that: He spins.

Each night *The O'Reilly Factor* wheels in a guest prepared to debate the host. A nice law professor in an elbow-patched jacket is set to discuss an obscenity law. This is a mistake, as O'Reilly quickly constructs a flimsy straw-man argument: "Do you really enjoy seeing pictures of Jesus Christ immersed in urine, Professor?" Then O'Reilly unleashes some verbal judo flips, leaving our scrappy academic flummoxed. It's pure magic.

It's silliness, but it's magic nonetheless.

We cannot say for sure whether O'Reilly plays fantasy football, but we're certain that he'd be a fearsome foe. Loofah or not, no one could instill doubt more quickly than O'Reilly. And if he were in the Bush League, he'd undoubtedly potshot players with question marks. Which is exactly what Thind and The Mick are doing to Kwame right now.

Kwame is doing his best to repel their verbal assault. And for what it's worth, he's probably right. Snagging Priest Holmes isn't any more of a gamble than taking a number of other top-tier running backs. But already, Thind is predicting a season-ending injury in week three.

"Stick a fork in him—he's done," says Thind.

Just like that, another manager has entered the No Spin Zone.

O'REILLY-ISMS

1. "Bill Moyers on PBS, he hides behind the label of objectivity. He's about as objective as Mao Tse-tung, all right. I mean he's a far-left bomb-thrower who actually runs a foundation that funds left-wing organizations. I mean, the guy's a joke. Get out of the news business, Bill."

2. "So who turns out for the screening of this movie *Fahrenheit 9/11* last night? You ready? Now, here are the celebrities that turn out. Here are the people who would turn out to see Joseph Goebbels convince you that Poland invaded the Third Reich. It's the same thing, by the way. Propaganda is propaganda."

3. "You want to have two guys making out in front of your four-year-old? It's okay with them. A guy smoking a joint, blowing the smoke into your little kid's face? Okay with them. And I'm not exaggerating here. This is exactly what the secular movement stands for."

OTHER POSTDRAFT REACTIONS

1. **The Tinkering Reaction:** Manager who immediately wants to improve team through preseason free agency

2. **The "You drive a Hyundai, I drive a BMW" Reaction:** Manager who views other teams with utter disdain

3. **The Mr. Rogers Reaction:** Manager who's complimentary about every single team in the league
4. **The Helter Skelter Reaction:** Manager in four different fantasy leagues who can't remember which players are on which team
5. **The Conflicted Hometowner Reaction:** Manager who realizes that his core fantasy players will all face his hometown NFL team

6

<< SOWING DOUBT IN >>
THE FIRST-PICK DIALOGUE

THE FOLLOWING CONVERSATION OCCURRED BETWEEN AL
Lopez (screen name: ElMatador1) and Adam Goldman (screen name: DrToes) September seventh, the day after the draft. Goldman, who continues to dislike his team, clings to his last bastion of hope: LaDainian Tomlinson, the first pick in the draft and one of the truly elite players. *At least* he has LaDainian. Lopez, largely for sport, decides to chip away at that last vestige of hope.

> **ElMatador1 (5:07:18 PM):** Was tough figuring out who to take first, huh?
>
> **DrToes (5:07:43 PM):** No. LaDainian Tomlinson, or LT2 as I call him, is cash money. Super-reliable.
>
> **ElMatador1 (5:07:58 PM):** LT2 has questions. Everyone has questions.
>
> **DrToes (5:10:03 PM):** Not sure I understand . . .
>
> **ElMatador1 (5:10:08 PM):** I'd look hard at his stats. Quite hard.
>
> **DrToes (5:10:19 PM):** Chuckle.
>
> **ElMatador1 (5:11:00 PM):** Seriously, I don't at all understand why he was the consensus number one.

DrToes (5:11:32 PM): Consistency, mainly. In his prime. Runs and catches.

ElMatador1 (5:12:37 PM): Ah, yes. But his number of touches is interesting to me. Name the number of backs with over 400 rushing and receiving attempts who haven't seen a reduced workload the following year.

DrToes (5:15:20 PM): Dunno. LT2 has had 2,100 and 2,400 combined yards the last two years. 15 and 17 touchdowns.

ElMatador1 (5:16:08 PM): I just don't quite get why a guy who's had 400+ touches and (relatively) low yards per carry is a shoo-in.

ElMatador1 (5:16:54 PM): There are a number of guys who I could easily see having better years.

DrToes (5:17:30 PM): Perhaps. But LT2's floor seems fairly capped. Which pretty much can't be said about any other running back.

ElMatador1 (5:19:41 PM): Don't really see his floor as lower than, say, Ahman Green. Or even Deuce. If they're healthy, those guys will get at least 1,800 combined yards and 10 touches.

DrToes (5:20:32 PM): So you say.

ElMatador1 (5:22:33 PM): I guess LT2 might have a slightly higher TD floor. But I suspect his touchdowns will go down significantly this year.

DrToes (5:22:38 PM): Based on what?

ElMatador1 (5:22:43 PM): For one thing, SD is developing other weapons. I just think they'll be more balanced.

DrToes (5:23:27 PM): That often helps a running back, not hurts. You could argue there are more weapons to spread the ball around to, and the offense will score more b/c there are more weapons. Both of which I think are true.

ElMatador1 (5:25:21 PM): Could be. The other thing I don't like about LT2 is he's rather hit-or-miss.

ElMatador1 (5:25:26 PM): His big games are huge.

ElMatador1 (5:25:32 PM): But he's really quite inconsistent.

ElMatador1 (5:26:33 PM): You still there?

DrToes (5:27:32 PM): Sorry. Back. Dealing with some patient issues.

DrToes (5:27:47 PM): To your point . . . not sure what your point is. As I said earlier, LT2 scored 15 and 17 touchdowns. How inconsistent could he be?

ElMatador1 (5:28:10 PM): Not my point. At least, I don't think it is. I'm talking about yardage. I think touchdowns are a little random. But could easily see him getting fewer touchdowns next year.

ElMatador1 (5:28:15 PM): At any rate, I got to get out of here.

DrToes (5:29:01 PM): Again, the guy is automatic. He's never scored less than 11. Playing in a truly rotten, rotten offense.

ElMatador1 (5:29:11 PM): Right. Which brings me back to my main point.

DrToes (5:29:17 PM): I have no idea what your main point is.

ElMatador1 (5:29:59 PM): Point is how often have you seen a guy have three straight years of 400+ touches not lose steam? There's sort of a law of averages thing.

DrToes (5:30:11 PM): So, can you confirm those numbers? Not sure I've seen them anywhere.

ElMatador1 (5:30:22 PM): Yeah, got them around here somewhere. I'll send you the link later.

ElMatador1 (5:30:25 PM): Anyway, gotta run.

DrToes (5:31:19 PM): I don't get that last point. But doesn't strike me as a big concern.

ElMatador1 (5:31:21 PM): Last point is, if you have that many carries, your body starts to wear down at some point.

This results in lower productivity. Or greater injury, or both. Objectively speaking, LT2 could be in trouble.

DrToes (5:32:04 PM): Objectively speaking, indeed. I guess that would be a bigger concern were he not 25 and in his prime, and had he not been a rock thus far.

ElMatador1 (5:32:34 PM): Well, I have concerns. But I probably would have taken him too. I love LT2. The guy plays like Sonic the Hedgehog. Incredibly fun to watch.

DrToes (5:33:45 PM): I'm exhausted. When all is said and done, I'm glad to have LT2 on Team Goyim. He's my franchise player.

ElMatador1 (5:34:12 PM): Yeah, I probably would have taken him too.

DrToes (5:34:15 PM): You would have?

ElMatador1 (5:34:17 PM): I guess.

DrToes (5:34:25 PM): Oh. What were we talking about, then?

ElMatador1 (5:34:30 PM): Not really sure. But I gotta run.

ElMatador1 (5:34:31 PM): I'm out like sauerkraut.

DrToes (5:34:46 PM): Later.

7

<< SUNDAY CALLINGS >>

ON A CLEAR AND BREEZY SUNDAY A MOMENT OF TRUTH IS fast approaching. Men have prepared for this moment for months.

Week One. Two words that generate both excitement and anxiety.

The golden days of summer will soon become a distant memory as fantasy managers descend into dark, musty sports bars. Daytime activities change, habits are set, and expectations for socially acceptable behavior are lowered.

But first, there's one final test. Much as the wildebeests of the African Serengeti Plain are forced to cross alligator-infested waters at the end of their long migration, fantasy managers must make one final push to reach their sanctuary. Significant hurdles remain. Traverse these obstacles, and afternoons of football-watching, trash-talking, and chicken wings await.

Fail, and all is for naught.

THE UNFORTUNATE MORNING COMMITMENT

Prashun Thind has been preparing for Week One since late July. A veritable urban warrior, he's outfitted with the latest iPAQ Pocket PC mobile device—a key competitive edge, he reminds himself. Prash is also a cell phone holster guy. He keeps his backup within quick reach should he receive an important secondary call.

Ninety minutes before kickoff he methodically punches buttons, takes calls, and only occasionally glances up at oncoming foot traffic. As his jaunt up Broadway continues, his cell phone rings to Mos Def's "Miss Fat Booty."

"Allo," Thind says in a faux–British accent.

"Prashun, this is Kwame."

"Yo, what's up, homey? How's my shizza?"

"Prash, I need to make this quick, as my signal is fading. I'm coordinating a bar to watch the games. We're hitting the Bump-N-Run, all right?"

"Absolutely, bro. That sounds—" But before he can finish, Kwame's phone cuts out. A few moments later Prash's phone rings again. "Yo, Kwame. That bar works great for me. And check this out. You gotta hear these new moan tones. They're from porn stars—how sweet is that?"

There's silence on the other end. Then audible throat clearing. "Prashun, this is your mother."

"Oh. Hello, mother."

"We're coming out of the Holland Tunnel. Are you still joining us for brunch?"

"Um, yes. I'll see you shortly."

Prash curses silently. There it is: the unfortunate morning commitment. A complicating factor in his week one pre-game preparation.

He shuffles up to the entrance of Indus Valley, his father's favorite restaurant. His parents are waiting inside. The Thind family take their seats in silence.

Prash checks his watch. Sixty minutes until kickoff.

"How's the job going?" his father asks. "Aren't you due a promotion?"

"Well . . ." Prash takes a bite of his Tikka Masala.

"Are you dating?" his mother asks. "Is there a special woman in your life?" Prash looks down at his plate and pokes at some cooked yams.

"You know," Mrs. Thind continues, "The Chandrasekhars' daughter, Priya, is still very interested in meeting you. She's a terrific clay-court tennis player."

Thind shakes his head and excuses himself from the table. He darts into the restroom and whips out his . . . HP iPAQ Pocket PC. Prashun pulls up a flood of sports-wire reports and discovers that disaster has struck the Thindianapolis Colts. The one thing he feared: His starting tight end, Dallas Clark's injury status has changed from "probable" to "questionable."

TOP FIVE PLAYERS LISTED AS "QUESTIONABLE"

1. Fred Taylor
2. Plaxico Burress
3. Michael Bennett
4. Warrick Dunn
5. Steve McNair

This is not how any manager wants to start the season. Prash can already envision his postgame press release:

> The Thindianapolis Colts were left reeling after the late scratch of starting tight end, Dallas Clark. Fans are already questioning feckless team manager, Thindy Infante, over his inability to make timely personnel moves on account of brunch with his meddling parents.

He returns to the table.

"Prashun, what's wrong with you?" Mrs. Thind asks. "You seem troubled."

"Enough of this, Prashun," says Mr. Thind. "Let me be clear. We're concerned about you."

Prash is glancing down at his iPAQ, checking other injury reports.

"We think you've lost focus. That's unacceptable. You've worked too hard to be so listless. *We've* worked too hard for you to be this listless."

Prashun checks his watch; it's twelve thirty. Exit-strategy time.

"Mom and Dad, you guys make perfect sense. I appreciate your insights. But unfortunately, I have to deal with the, um, Penske File[10] at work. Thanks for brunch. I'll call you tomorrow."

"Prashun, we want to talk to you—"

"I would love that, but I can't abandon my work, now can I?"

His father opens his mouth and then closes it.

Thind tosses his napkin down on the table as his mother looks on confused. Yes, Prash loves his parents. And yes, he respects them too. But he won't miss the start of the season on account of their meddling. So he exits the restaurant and breaks into a full sprint to the nearest subway station.

TOO BLACK, TOO STRONG

In Murray Hill, Kwame Jones is trying to find solace in the last known refuge for men—the sports bar. As he steps inside the Bump-N-Run, he's overcome by reassuring sites, sounds, and smells.

In the corner sits Dawgpound Dave spouting off about how the Browns will finally produce a 1,000-yard rusher. At the bar Cowboy Hank is carefully laying out his lone-star towel. In the back Eagle Eric is making fluttering arm motions and inexplicably wearing a Lenny Dykstra jersey.

In the overwhelming darkness of the Bump-N-Run, Kwame feels

---

10. If ever there was a metaphor for the drudgery of corporate office work, thy name is Costanza and the Penske File.

relatively anonymous. But that doesn't mean he has it easy. For one thing, many have a beef with him because he's a fantasy player. Each week when he pulls out his matchups sheet, he's greeted with unmitigated disdain. Cowboy Hank calls him a "stat head," and Eagle Eric refers to him as a "slide-rule guy."

Kwame shakes them off. Even though he's the biggest guy in the bar, he doesn't like to make trouble. So when Dawgpound Dave asks him where Cleveland's going this year, Kwame just smiles and responds, "To the Super Bowl."

"Aight, bro," Dave says, clapping him on the back. Kwame hates it when people speak to him this way, in semi-Ebonics. "Way to go, dawg."

GUYS WE LIKE AT SPORTS BARS

1. Man who throws down his baseball cap whenever his team screws up
2. The guy who pats everyone on the back too roughly
3. The bartender who shouts, "If you're staying, you're buying a drink"
4. The loose cannon who screams "motherfucker" every ten minutes
5. The gambling addict who refers to his bets in "units"

For whatever reason, white guys have always been comfortable around Kwame. As a big African American he seems approachable. He's their man, their G., and sometimes he's their O.G.

The truth is that Kwame doesn't have any "street" in him. And he feels no particular affiliation to the East Si-i-i-de or the West Side. Perhaps this is because his parents, Joseph and Felicia, raised him in Evanston, Illinois, where they insisted that he speak the "King's English."

So when Eagle Eric asks how he feels about "my boy, McNabb,"

Kwame just mutters something about him being okay. "What, you like Vick? McNair? So who's your son, son?"

"I don't think I have son, son," Kwame says, smiling, "but I like watching all of those guys." Then he scratches his chin, coughs into his hand, and waits patiently for his friends to arrive.

A PRAYER FOR TORN ACLS

At eleven o'clock Schlots wakes up to catch the late mass at St. Benedict's. His mind flickers back and forth—he considers his week one starters, ponders God, then reconsiders his starters. On all counts Schlots is quite optimistic. God is good, and so are The Fat Minnesota Guys.

Much of his religious devotion stems from his childhood. Starting at the age of eight, he was an altar boy. But he was never molested. Father Thomas warned Schlots that if he didn't "hew to the straight and narrow," he'd never leave his hometown of Boulder Junction, Minnesota.

As it turns out, Father Thomas was right. Without his faith Schlots could have turned out like his friends. "Sloppy" Joe Henry lost his left forearm in a hunting accident when his brother mistook him for an elk. John "Hard Lump" Needham set the Open Pines County record with forty-five DUIs. And Ryan "Milky" Tosero sired four children before he turned twenty-two.[11]

Schlots's faith has continued into his adult life. Even after his wife has left him, he still attends church. He feels comfortable there.

As Schlots dresses, The Mick calls. "How does it feel to enter week one without a legitimate starting running back?"

Schlots responds, "How does it feel to enter week one without *your* backup running back, my boy James Mungro?" He hangs up, puts on

---

11. Schlots describes visiting Tosero's family as "watching *Lord of the Flies* set in a slightly unclean version of Costco." He also says that there's not a single day where at least one of Tosero's kids does not have a runny nose.

his Notre Dame football polo shirt, decides that it's slightly inappropriate for church, and throws on a Vikings jacket over it.

Five minutes later he shuffles down the block to St. Benedict's.

Once inside he goes to the far wall and lights votive candles. He lights a candle for Lou Holtz, and he lights a candle for his fantasy squad. He then lights a candle praying that Randy Moss goes for 120 yards and 2 touchdowns. Finally, he lights a candle praying that both of O'Brien's starting running backs go down with season-ending injuries.

This isn't exactly What-Would-Jesus-Do behavior, but Schlots feels as though he doesn't have a choice. He has The Mick's backup. If prayer helps at all, then why not ask JC for torn ACLs?

Schlots sits in a pew near the back. To his right are two women who resemble Statler and Waldorf. They're not very friendly to Schlots as he stumbles past them. He tries to focus on the sermon, but he's still running through his fantasy football prayers.

In front of him Father Alphonso—a thin man with veiny hands—is speaking today about scandal. "The wolf catcheth and scattereth the sheep," he says. Schlots pays attention for a while, but soon loses focus. He's looking for a sign: In ten minutes he'll need to finalize his lineup, and he's still not sure whether to start Plaxico Burress or Deion Branch at wide receiver.

He tries fighting the urge, the gnawing temptation, but finally he breaks down. He pulls out his cell phone and scans through his e-mail for a clue. But there's only this note from O'Brien: *"Mungro can go to hell."*

"Forgive him, Lord," Schlots whispers, "and please break Edge's kneecap."

The old women in his row are staring at him. Schlots smiles apologetically.

"Woe to the man who indulges in gossip," Father Alphonso says, and Schlots once again ponders his team. He'd planned on starting Plaxico Burress this week, but wait a minute . . . hadn't the star receiver demanded that he get more "touches" than Hines Ward? And hadn't Deion Branch—who is currently on Schlots's bench—said that he wanted to *avoid* scandal at all costs? And isn't Deion a Christian who wrote "PFJ"[12] on his wristband?

The sermon's running long. Schlots's phone vibrates. More O'Brien e-mails. (Damn him, in a manner of speaking.) Schlots has five minutes to make changes.

That's it, he thinks. The Lord has spoken: Schlots needs to bench Burress and get Branch into his lineup. So he scrambles over the old women on his way toward the door. As he's leaving, he hears one of them saying that it's a shame, a crying shame, to see a young man like that losing his faith.

THE CASSANDRA COMPACT

After hopping a plane from Los Angeles to New York, Al Lopez drifted off to sleep early Sunday morning, giddy with anticipation.

But at four in the morning his slumber was disturbed by a client, Cassandra Johnson. Cassandra is a dim-witted, talentless hack. She also happens to have D-size breasts, a penchant for slithering into all the hot parties, and a level of vapidity so extreme that she's viewed by the general public as cute and harmless. Much like her predecessor, Paris Hilton,[13] Cassandra has coined her own inane catchphrase ("Zesty!"), and everyone loves her all the more for it.

Except for when she calls people at four in the morning, bleating like a stuck pig. Then everyone, specifically Al Lopez, doesn't like her so much.

"Al, this is Cassandra. I'm in Rome; I just got in a fight with some I-talian assholes, and I'm scared. I have a split lip. What's this going to do to my face?"

"All right, calm down," Al's voice croaks, still only half-awake. "You

12. PFJ = "Play for Jesus"
13. The Jackie Robinson of talentless hacks.

may need stitches. You should go to the hospital. Get checked out."

"The hospital? Hospitals aren't open on Sundays."

Al pinches the bridge of his nose. "Um, no, hospitals *are* open on Sundays. That's in the event that people require medical care on a Sunday."

"Really? So it's not like the post office?"

Al sighs. "Listen, you should be fine. I'll call some of our people in Rome. They'll take you to the hospital."

He hangs up and returns to bed. Briefly he considers the fate of Cassandra Johnson, but soon his thoughts turn to matchups and statistics. He imagines his running backs having workmanlike games— 25 carries, 100 yards, 2 touchdowns. He takes one more pass through his starting lineup, and sees no major weaknesses.

Yep, I'm good to go, he thinks, before he falls back asleep.

The next morning he's awoken at nine thirty a.m. by his cell phone. Vanessa is touching base. "Al, the baby's running a fever; I'd love it if you could catch the next flight home."

This is an unanticipated leg-sweep. It's the start of the fantasy football season—the most exciting day of the year. If ever there were a time for Al to evade his wife's demands, this would be it. "Vanessa," he says, "I'd love to come home, but you know I have obligations in New York."

"Obligations on a Sunday, Al?"

"Yeah . . . I'm, uh, working." Al then throws out a flurry of reasons for why a flight out on Sunday isn't possible, none of which Vanessa particularly buys. Suddenly his phone beeps. He asks Vanessa to hold, and clicks over.

"Al? Cassandra. What up?"

"Oh, hey, Cassandra. How's your face?"

"It's all good. I'm already out at this dope new club. It's *très* zesty."

Another beep. Vanessa. "Alejandro, you're not going to be one of those fathers who ignores his children, are you? Please tell me that you aren't."

"Vanessa, I'm fully committed. But I have to go."

"I'll wait until you're done."

"What?"

"I'm waiting."

"Uh, right." Al clicks back over.

Cassandra's still talking, apparently unaware that she's been on hold. "Al, you seem distracted. Is everything all right?"

"I'm fine . . . fine." Al has no desire to get into it with Cassandra. So he changes the subject. "But it's the opening weekend of my fantasy football season. High stakes stuff. And I can't decide which defense to start—the Philadelphia Eagles or the Seattle Seahawks."

"Oh, I'd definitely take the Eagles over the Seahawks. Seahawks can't fly. You know, like ducks."

"Um, I think ducks *can* fly. Maybe you're thinking of penguins?"

"Oh. Maybe. Still, I like the Eagles. Go with them." With that, Cassandra hangs up, leaving a moderately flustered Al in her wake. Al checks his watch. He has two hours to set his roster, and dopey Cassandra has offered him as good a reason as any for choosing his starting defense.

Suddenly he remembers to check back in with his wife. He clicks over.

"It's started, hasn't it?"

"What's started?"

"Fantasy football season. It's started again, hasn't it?"

"Uh, honey—," Al says, and then he stops. There's no point in digging a bigger hole. "I'll call you before the late games—"

"Al—"

"Love you, honey, but I got to go."

OLD HABITS DIE HARD

On Sunday morning The Mick is proceeding through his long list of pre-game rituals.

He washes his Randall Cunningham coffee mug for the final time, and will not wash it again until season's end. He carefully puts on two pairs of tube socks and pushes his sweatshirt sleeves just past his forearms, where they must remain for the next ten hours for "good luck." He washes his hands and air-dries them—he won't use a towel. He plays House of Pain's "Jump Around," a song that he listens to only during the fall. He places the trading cards of his second-year wide receivers facedown on his kitchen table. He arranges them in an equilateral triangle.

BREAKOUT SECOND-YEAR WRS (FIRST YEAR/SECOND YEAR)

1. Plaxico Burress (273 yards, 2 TDs to 1,008 yards, 6 TDs)
2. Jerry Rice (927 yards, 3 TDs to 1,570 yards, 15 TDs)
3. Torry Holt (788 yards, 6 TDs to 1,635 yards, 6 TDs)
4. Chad Johnson (329 yards, 1 TD to 1,166 yards, 5 TDs)

He puts on his "Chronic" cap and tilts it at a forty-five-degree angle. He watches three, and only three, rounds of SportsCenter on mute. Whenever he sees Chris Berman, he whispers a different player's nickname: Rich "Loose" Gannon, Amani "It's Not A" Toomer, and so on. Finally he turns on his computer's stat tracker, pounds his desk five times, and says, "Let's go to work."

The Mick has done the same exact thing during week one for the last five seasons. This is his routine, his ritual. It's what makes him whole.

TIKI CAN'T WAIT

The aroma of flowers wafts through the air. Hushed classical music plays in the background. A calming trickle of water flows from a small indoor fountain. Adam Goldman stands, arms crossed, surveying the room.

How on earth did he end up at *this* place on *this* day? The stiff grip of Margaret Ming jostles him from his reverie. She leads Adam down a fern-covered aisle to the front desk, and jingles a miniature bell.

"That won't be necessary, Ms. Ming," says a deep French-accented voice from behind them. "I heard you two come in."

Adam and Margaret wheel around. But Adam sees no one. "Hello, my darling," coos Margaret as she bends down for a hug.

Adam follows her downward movement, and quickly identifies the diminutive owner of the deep voice. It appears their wedding planner is a dwarf. His hand is extended, awaiting a handshake.

"Hello, Adam. I'm Hedges. Your wedding planner." He is a meticulously dressed fellow, down to a matching tangerine necktie and kerchief.

"Hedges, you say?"

"Yes, Hedges DeVoe." He forces a smile. "Now then, shall we get started? You have a December date, so I'm thinking we'd go with somber browns and silent tans."

Adam begins to tune out. The date of their wedding remains a touchy subject. Initially they'd settled on September third, Labor Day weekend. This, of course, was a devastating setback for Adam, as it would have prevented him from participating in the Bush League draft.

Fortunately, Aunt Goldie, his mother's pushy South Florida sister, said that Labor Day weekend wouldn't work. Her son Daniel had his bar mitzvah scheduled.

Now, Adam couldn't care less whether or not his aunt Goldie, who is guaranteed to re-gift a tacky Lucite serving platter, and his scrappy cousin Daniel, who repeatedly asks Adam to take him to a "titty" bar, even come. But Adam was happy to have his relatives fall on the Margaret Ming wedding-date grenade. So September third was struck from the books, and a new date of December twentieth was set.

Adam's Bush League run remained secure.

The downside to this victory was that Adam had essentially forfeited whatever shred of leverage he had going into this process. Which is why a dwarf named Hedges is leading him around a fancy store mere hours before the start of week one.

"So let's focus on your wedding cake," Hedges says. "Where would you like to start?"

Margaret begins working down her meticulously prepared list. Adam attempts to listen and contribute. But everything sounds muffled, like the teacher from *Peanuts*—"Wha, wha wha, wha wha wha."

GREAT PEANUTS CHARACTERS

1. Franklin. Sole African-American.
2. Peppermint Patty and Marcie. Overcame longstanding lesbian rumors.
3. Spike. Represented Needles, California.
4. Joe Schlabotnik. Charlie Brown's baseball hero.
5. Charlotte Braun. Louder and more obnoxious than Lucy, she only appeared in ten strips.

The reality of marriage further dawns on him. He's about to become a husband, but he's by no means in control. Ms. Ming will be the signal-caller, the one running the two-minute offense. For the wedding planning in particular she'll be calling audibles with greater frequency than Peyton Manning against the Pats.

Again, the commanding Hedges DeVoe shakes Adam from his daze. Margaret is very fond of the three-layered cake on display at a nearby table. What does Adam think?

Adam, unprepared, mutters, "How about one of those ice cream cakes you get at Baskin-Robbins? Tastes just as good, but much cheaper."

Margaret gasps.

Hedges shakes his head slowly. "No, I'm sorry. That won't do, Adam. But good contribution. I'm glad you're staying involved."

Adam's ready to tap out. "Listen, it seems like you're in good hands with Hedges. I'm cool with whatever you do. So I'm, um, going to head out."

"Adam, this is not the type of involvement we discussed. This is important to me. This is important to *us*. I thought we'd agreed that you'd put your fantasy football nonsense on hold this year?"

"Tiki's calling me."

"Adam, Tiki can wait."

"No, honey, Tiki *can't* wait. You know I agree with all your choices. I trust your decisions. My work here is done."

Adam spins around and heads for the door. Even though he'll take a hit for this, he has to go. He's late, but he's shaken loose now, and he's running to daylight.

<< SCENES FROM THE BAR >>

12:42 P.M.

Schlots, O'Brien, Thind, and Lopez enter the Bump-N-Run. Kwame, already seated, raises his hand. They shuffle over. The guys shake hands and bump chests.

"You ready?"

"I couldn't sleep last night I was so geeked."

"Dude, I'm double-geeked. I've been looking at my lineup all morning; it gives me the chills."

"My lineup's tight, real tight."

"Everyone's tight!" Thind says. "Tight, tight, tight!"

Other patrons look dismissively at the Bush League table.

"Thind, keep it cool," Kwame says.

"Roger that!" Thind attempts to bump fists. He wants to "punch it out."

Kwame stares at him, then sits.

12:46 P.M.

Schlots whips out a white towel with the words BUSH LEAGUE CHAMPION printed on it. Kwame unfolds his matchup sheet.

Thind "docks" his Pocket PC and "drops mad science" on the Vegas line.

12:48 P.M.

A drunk guy in yellow and black sweatpants approaches the table and yells, "Steelers, sissy-boys, Steelers!"

Schlots responds, "Bush League, motherfucker, Bush League!"

The stranger takes a step backward, shakes his head, and walks away.

Thind pats Schlots on the back.

12:49 P.M.

Tricia, a long-time Bumpette, says, "Drinks?" Schlots orders a pitcher of Michelob. It's unclear whether this is for himself or for the group. So Kwame orders a second pitcher. The Mick, a bit out of sorts, asks for a dirty martini.

"The Mick seems a bit fancy this morning," Schlots says.

Thind asks whether The Mick will be "having caviar with his chili fries." The Mick gives a "What?" look, then caves and orders a Bud.

12:57 P.M.

Thind tries to convince the bartender that the main screen should be showing the Saints and not the Bills because "Buffalo is where fantasy studs go to die." In response, the bartender hands him a basket of peanuts. Thind scampers back to the table.

12:59 P.M.

There's much clapping and head-nodding as kickoff approaches. "It's on, baby!" Thind says.

"Yeah, baby, it's on," Schlots says.

"We're ready, baby," Lopez adds. "We . . . are . . . ready. Give us our football, give us our football *now!*"

INTERESTING FANTASY TEAMS

1. Broncos. Faces papier-mâché defenses in the AFC West. Consistently fields RBs with Madden-esque moves.
2. Chiefs. Holmes, Johnson, and the rest of the offense almost created as a prototypical fantasy football team.
3. Vikings. Three receivers, three running backs, two tight ends, and one QB owned by Bush League managers. All under the management of the truly dopey Mike Tice.
4. Rams. As long as Coach Martz is at the helm, the Rams will always—*always*—run up the score.

TERRIBLE FANTASY TEAMS

1. Browns. We challenge you to name one player on this team who's had three decent fantasy years. Seriously. Name one. We dare you.
2. 49ers. Arguably the only team in the NFL without a legitimate fantasy starter. And no, Kevan Barlow does *not* count. Never has a dynasty gone south so quickly.
3. Bears. Mike Ditka would be spinning in his grave.

1:00 P.M.

Kickoff. Not a soul utters a word.

1:03 P.M.

Adam Goldman hustles into the Bump-N-Run with sweat pouring off his brow. The rest of the group, well aware of the cause for his delay, smile knowingly. As Goldman approaches the table, The Mick stands and pantomimes holding and striking a gong, complete with the soft mallet meets metallic surface *Bwwwongggg!* sound.

Goldman motions for a beer.

1:08 P.M.

Peyton Manning hits Marvin Harrison on a quick out-route, and Harrison jets 77 yards for a touchdown—securing 7 points for the yardage covered, 6 points for reaching the end zone, and 2 bonus points for the long touchdown.

One play. Fifteen points. Priceless.

Thind, who proudly (though unimpressively) drafted Harrison in the first round, bursts out of his chair, and says, "That's how we do this. I'm telling you, that's how we do this."

Others drink their beers and pretend not to notice.

1:33 P.M.

Kwame in his annual week one taunt to Goldman notes that "Team Goyim's wide-receiving corps seems to lack depth."

Goldman, in his annual week one response, says he "liked Wayne Chrebet's route-running in camp," and looks "for him to have a bounce-back year."

Kwame hesitates, then asks, "Bounce-back from what?"

1:36 P.M.

Thind is the only one watching the Dolphins game. He erupts in a devious little cheer when Chris Chambers nabs a 20-yard catch.

"That's my boy," Thind says. But the replay shows that it wasn't Chambers. Instead it was the rather unimpressive Derrius Thompson.

"Hey, Prash," Lopez says, "is Thompson your boy?"

No answer.

"Is he?"

"No."

"Say it. Say it, so we don't have to hear your little bird-chirps all afternoon."

"No," Thind says, "Thompson is not my boy."

DEFINITIVELY MEDIOCRE FANTASY PLAYERS

1. Wayne Chrebet. The Scott Baio of wide receivers.
2. Marty Booker. Terrible name makes it hard to take him seriously.
3. Itula Mili. Or any Polynesian player.
4. Ricky Proehl. Makes the tough "over the middle" token white-guy catches for 7 yards a pop.
5. Jay Fiedler. A popular pick at the annual Yeshiva draft.
6. Troy Hambrick. Emmitt Smith, if Emmitt Smith were never good.
7. Todd Pinkston, James Thrash, and any other wide receiver on the NFC East carousel.
8. Boo Williams. Fat and peepless.
9. Antowain Smith. 2.9 yards and a cloud of dust.
10. Koy Detmer. "Giddyup" TD celebration move is the NFL's most extravagant relative to talent.

1:38 P.M.

Ron Dayne enters the Giants game. O'Brien starts cheering for him, but only because he wants to anger Goldman, whose starter, Tiki Barber, risks losing carries to Dayne.

"Here comes Thunder," O'Brien says. "Thunder and Lightning—it's back this year." Dayne lines up behind Kurt Warner. "Go, Thunder, go." Dayne takes the handoff. "Come on, Thunder."

Dayne runs straight into the line.

No gain.

"Looks like Thunder isn't primed for a big year," Goldman says, smiling. Barber reenters the game, and Dayne trudges off to the sideline.

"We'll see about that," The Mick says, but his voice is hollow.

This rumor—that Dayne would actually be a player—was driven by pointless, relentless, and circular message-board speculation. But like many preseason rumors, this one is DOA in the first quarter of Week One.

1:41 P.M.

Schlots, having made quick work of his beer, belches a table-rattling burp and asks for another pitcher. He then rubs his stomach, takes his hat off, and rubs his head. Prash glances down at his barely touched pint, and takes two large gulps.

1:54 P.M.

Goldman lets loose with the first official angry outburst of the season when *his* LaDainian Tomlinson breaks through the line and begins jitterbugging 45 yards to the house. He slows down, however, as he nears the end zone, and is tripped up from behind at the 2-yard line.

On the ensuing play, quarterback Drew Brees plunges in for the touchdown. A dramatic twelve-point swing has occurred—from 6 sure ones for Team Goyim to 6 lucky ones for The Fat Minnesota Guys.

Schlots announces that he likes "Brees's scrambleability" and thinks he's "capable of matching Vick's rushing TD production this season." The others at the table chuckle and shake their heads. Goldman stands up and begins pacing around the bar, hands on hips.

MOST-FRUSTRATING FANTASY PLAYS

1. Your running back limps off the field during the opening possession with a "chest contusion." Five minutes later Tony Siragusa announces that your player won't return to the game.
2. Your quarterback scrambles, chucks a wounded duck, gets picked, then flails on an open-field tackle. Naturally he misses. And hurts his throwing hand in the process.
3. Your opponent's running back gets stopped behind the line of scrimmage, churns his leg, breaks free, then rumbles for a long TD.
4. In a red zone situation your running back goes straight up the gut two times and is stopped; then, on third down, the quarterback throws an easy slant to your opponent's wide receiver.
5. Your defense is pitching a shutout in the fourth quarter when a scrappy kick-returner darts through an initial wave of tacklers, leaving the kicker exposed as the last man back. Your kicker meekly tries to trip the returner with a soccer slide tackle.
6. Your stud running back busts loose for a 50-yard scamper. He's in the end zone, pumping his fist . . . but wait—there's a flag on the play.
7. Your wide receiver catches a long bomb. But on instant replay it's revealed that his second foot was out of bounds.
8. On third-and-long your kicker is shown preparing to chip in an easy field goal. But he never gets the chance because the QB on his team is sacked for a 15-yard loss.
9. Your quarterback has rushed for 22 yards on the day, producing 2 crucial fantasy points. With seconds left in the game he proceeds to down the ball twice to run out the clock. He loses 4 yards, wiping out your bonus points.
10. Your defense sacks the quarterback and forces a fumble. A superfat defensive lineman scoops up the ball, and instead of lateraling it to a speedy linebacker 2 feet from him, he lumbers toward the end zone. After he runs out of gas, he's tackled at the 4-yard line, robbing you of an easy defensive touchdown.

2:30 P.M.

At halftime, chicken wings, nachos, and, strangely, lentil soup orders are placed. Goldman asks Tricia (the Bumpette) if he can order a hamburger, but without the bun.

Tricia asks if he would like a lime spritzer with that.

He says a spritzer would be great.

She says that she was joking.

Thind asks her to "punch it out."

She declines.

2:37 P.M.

The Broncos have the ball on the 3-yard line. This is big-time red zone territory. The ever-reliable Denver running game is about to punch in another rushing touchdown.

Fantasy managers throughout the Bump-N-Run begin shouting. "Give the ball to Quentin Griffin!" "No, dish it to Mike Andersen!" "No, give it to Tatum Bell!"

But then quarterback Jake Plummer drops back, rolls right, and flips it to third-string tight end Patrick Hape, who scuttles in for the touchdown. FOXSports provides a close-up of a grinning, rosy-cheeked Mike Shanahan.

"Damn you, Skeletor!" someone shouts.

"He screwed me again," says another.

"He's the devil. Shanahan is the devil."

3:19 P.M.

Goldman checks his cell phone. Lopez checks his BlackBerry. They both have messages from their ladies. They both exhale through clenched lips.

During a commercial break Schlots announces that he's growing a mustache. "Kind of one of those Dennis Eckersley or *Magnum, P.I.*–type 'staches," he adds. "Just to change things up. Give me a new look."

"That's inspired," notes Lopez.

Prash asks whether Schlots will be wearing the accompanying assless chaps with his mustache. Schlots doesn't respond. Lopez, however, says that the mustache is making a huge comeback and Schlots is ahead of his time. Schlots, confused, nods in semi-agreement.

MOST-INSPIRED PRO ATHLETE MUSTACHES

1. Rollie Fingers—earned him a Rolaids commercial
2. James "Buddha" Edwards—precursor to NBA's Zen fashion trends
3. Joe Namath—reminiscent of high school mustaches
4. "Pistol" Pete Maravich—prototypical seventies look
5. Jake Plummer—oddly suggesting a new maturity in his game

4:45 P.M.

Michael Bennett, The Bitter Drafter's lone starting running back, goes down with a severely sprained ankle. Lesley Visser[14] provides a non-committal, nonmedical update on Bennett's status. He could be out for six weeks, or he could come back in the next series—Lesley's not sure.

O'Brien immediately calls The Bitter Drafter. "Tough break, bro."

"There will be hell to pay for this," says The Bitter Drafter. "Hell to pay."

---

14. Not to be confused with Lesley Stahl, Lisa Leslie, or any variety of other sideline roving female "reporters"—Suzy Kolber, Pam Oliver, and, possibly, Roller Girl.

5:19 P.M.

Through two quarters Priest Holmes has racked up 130 yards and 3 touchdowns. "Just another day at the office," Kwame says. "Priest punched in, and now he's doing his job. Kwame Jones, Inc., rolling strong."

5:23 P.M.

Despite having three Cardinals on his team, Thind finds himself unable to watch their game. "It's like watching the CFL," he says, before rifling through his Pocket PC to check Marcel Shipp's stats.

5:30 P.M.

The CBS Sports stat tracker scrolls across the bottom of the Bump-N-Run's many television screens. Fantasy managers stop following the live game action and focus intently on the litany of names and numbers.

Curtis Martin has had a big day so far. A pleasant surprise. Duce Staley has not. A bitter disappointment.

Fantasy managers are furiously scribbling down their players' stats, tallying points, estimating whether they're ahead or behind.

5:45 P.M.

Fatigue sets in. Lopez, tired and fading fast, slumps over and grabs some quick shut-eye. For his troubles Kwame places an empty plastic beer cup on Lopez's head. Thind, kid-brother-like, follows suit and places a cup of hot sauce under Lopez's nose.

5:57 P.M.

The Mick notices that both of The Hydra's quarterbacks are playing against each other. "It's the freaking Hydra Bowl," he says.

6:07 P.M.

Dante Hall, return man extraordinaire, shakes loose for his obligatory kickoff return for a touchdown. This is an incredibly exciting play. None of the guys have him on their roster as he's merely a scrappy fleet of foot special-teamer who insists on making an *X Factor* sign. But they appreciate the magnificence of this play.

High fives are exchanged all around.

6:31 P.M.

At the center of the table rests what appears to be a devoured animal carcass. In reality it is an unseemly pile of chicken wing bones—some picked clean, others with residual chicken gristle clinging stubbornly to cartilage.

6:43 P.M.

Lopez notices that The Death Maiden has the high score for week one. "Jesus, guys, she's beating us with a stick."

6:53 P.M.

As the afternoon games end, Schlots is gulping beer straight out of the pitcher. The last suds collect on his ruddy chin.

6:59 P.M.

Thind asks if anyone wants to stick around for the ESPN Sunday-night game. He's met with a string of murmurs: "need to get home," "got to get a jump on the week," and "have to water plants."

Darkness falls. Bush League combatants stagger out of the Bump-N-Run after a solid six hours of "work."

Goldman rubs his eyes and shivers.

O'Brien bunny-hops up and down, trying to get a little blood back in his legs.

"Good effort today, gentlemen," Kwame says.

Everyone exchanges handshakes, and parts ways.

Only sixteen weeks remain.

<< REQUEST FOR >>
A RULE CHANGE

EACH YEAR AT LEAST ONE BUSH LEAGUE RULE IS ADDED, tweaked, or eliminated. Ideally any rule changes are resolved prior to the start of the season. Sometimes, however, they are not, and a rare bit of league coordination and diplomacy is required.

This year a question has been raised over quarterback scoring. An obligatory e-mail chain ensues.

From: Jones, Kwame
Sent: Wednesday, September 15, 2004 10:15 AM
To: Bush League Mail List
Subject: QB Points

It appears that, just like congress, we pushed through a scoring measure before the draft that was so full of compromise that nothing came out of it but a few choice sound bites, a photo op, and a blistering editorial in the *Wall Street Journal* condemning the pervasive, combative nature of this league.

The QB scoring rule adopted ("railroaded" to some) just prior to the draft was intended to smooth out QB scoring this year, to make it more in line with RB/WR/TE scoring. That is, each yard is additive. As it was implemented, the rule makes no distinction between 251 yards and 274 yards, as these are between 25-point break points. Changing to a smoothing mechanism (i.e., .04 points/yard) would not alter anyone's Week One score by more than a fraction of a point, by definition, but would be more in the spirit of what we're attempting to accomplish.

Separately, some folks (or rather one folk, our resident miserablist) have suggested that .05 points/yard (based on 1 point per 20 yards, not 25, for those of you in the legal field) would be more appropriate. The latter may well be a more suitable change for next year, given that the point totals were agreed to on the call *before* the draft, and it would change a few scores, and one game result (coincidentally, the result of the proposer).

Therefore, I put it to you to decide on the first issue, whether we should have smoothing or maintain the break points. I'm also open to comments on the second, but unless there is overwhelming support for the scoring change, I would suggest we table that. At the very least, that would have to be enacted on a going forward basis, not retroactively, in the spirit of fairness.

Your thoughts are appreciated, notionally.

Kwame Jones

From: O'Brien, Chris
Sent: Wednesday, September 15, 2004 10:38 AM
To: Bush League Mail List
Subject: Re: QB Points

Kwame:

First of all, surprisingly, I'm not the miserablist (great word).

Second, I'm in favor of the smoothing for sure.

Third, I think I'm (moderately) in favor of the scoring change—here's why:

On the call, I suggested that 1 pt for every 25 yards is the fantasy football standard, which is true. But it's also the case that QBs in traditional fantasy leagues get 4 points per touchdown, which doesn't happen in the Bush League. The net effect of the railroad change is that outstanding QB performances are dampened—200 yards for a QB is a bad/mediocre day, but would get you 8 points. 300 yards is a great day, but only gets you 12. And you don't make that up (really) with touchdowns because they're only worth 3 points.

Shifting from 25 yards per point to 20 yards therefore makes sense. In all cases, I don't think that the scoring change should be made retroactively.

The Mick

From: Thind, Prashun
Sent: Wednesday, September 15, 2004 11:18 AM
To: Bush League Mail List
Subject: Re: QB Points

Kwame,

I agree with The Mick's analysis. I don't think the scoring change would have materially altered anyone's draft strategy; which, in nonlegal parlance, means that it's not really that important.

Thindy Infante

From: Goldman, Adam
Sent: Wednesday, September 15, 2004 11:37 AM
To: Bush League Mail List
Subject: Re: QB Points

In the interest of full disclosure, Thind should have let you all know that portions of that response were researched and written by a team of 12 lawyers sitting in a dark room somewhere in Mumbai, India (although, curiously, you can reach them at a 646 phone number, should you be interested in employing their services).

For my part, first off let me thank Kwame and The Mick for doing the math on all this—while I can't speak for other Bush League managers, I know that I had already started to remove my shoes and socks to figure out the net effect. Secondly, I can say with certainty: Who cares? I'm happy to write a medical opinion assuring interested parties that this scoring change will not affect your health—or, for that matter, the outcome of any game played in our league. (Of course, if you are interested in such an opinion, you should know two things (i) my standard rate is $625/hour and (ii) medical opinions are worthless.)

I'm happy to (i) vote in favor of the smoothing change for consistency's sake and (ii) start using the "new" system in week 2. Then again, if nobody wants the change, that's fine too. Wow, you know, democracy really is empowering— together we can make a difference.

On a completely unrelated but equally irrelevant note: I'd like to announce that I am selling the naming rights to Team Goyim's stadium. Please submit all bids and name suggestions to the home office in Sioux City, Iowa.

Adam

From: Lopez, Alejandro
Sent: Wednesday, September 15, 2004 11:51 AM
To: Bush League Mail List
Subject: Re: QB Points

Y'know something?
We've all been clamoring (for years) for Goldman to

"say something once in a while," "be more engaged," "participate," and "change your freaking team name." And now the guy actually takes the time out of his busy day to write something out, you know, to *contribute,* and what happens?

It sucks.

I can't wait to see what the new stadium name will be . . . I've got $20 bucks on "Stadium Goyim."

Al

From: Goldman, Adam
Sent: Wednesday, September 15, 2004 12:12 PM
To: Bush League Mail List
Subject: Re: QB Points

I had no idea we got graded on this stuff. Sorry. I'll try harder, unless I have permission to go back into my season-long cocoon?

Stadium Goyim does sort of have a nice ring to it.

From: Schlotterbeck, John
Sent: Wednesday, September 15, 2004 2:44 PM
To: Bush League Mail List
Subject: Re: QB Points

Wait, what's going on with the quarterbacks? If someone drafted Bledsoe, does that number get multiplied by 1,000? And do I get points for fumbles?

By the way, of the 43 daily football e-mails I receive, these are by far the most entertaining. Speaking of entertainment, Goldman is really a funny guy. You just have to get past the medical talk, the mulligans, and his pre–Margaret Ming addiction to JDate.

<< EARLY SEASON >>
STRATEGIES

WIN . . . LOSE . . . THE FIRST WEEK OF FANTASY FOOTBALL
is just a number. It's not even data; it's datum, singular—a funny
word.

The difference between going 1–0 and 0–1 is relatively small. But
by the end of Week Three you have data. You have trends. Some teams
are taking off. Others are crashing faster than MC Hammer's career.

Certain realities must be acknowledged. Yes, you can overcome a
0–3 start and still win a championship. But moves must be made, and
made quickly. Similarly, it's possible that a 3–0 team can flail, but it's
not likely.

Either way, one thing is certain—your in-season strategy is largely
based on where you stand after Week Three. It's the point in the season where boys become men, men start panicking, and the guppies
swim to shelter.

THE ROPE-A-DOPE STRATEGY

In 1974 Muhammad Ali unveiled his celebrated "Rope-a-Dope"
against George Foreman during their "Rumble in the Jungle."

The idea behind this strategy was simple: Ali let Foreman wail on him for six rounds, falling back against the ropes to absorb the punishing blows, encouraging Foreman to continue lumbering forward. Round after round the hard-hitting Foreman pounded Ali's body.

Even Don King cringed.

ONLY IN AMERICA: DON KING QUOTES

1. "I'm a promoter of the people for the people and by the people, and my magic lies in my people ties. I'm a promoter of America. I'm American people. You know what I mean? So therefore, uh, do not send for who the bell tolls 'cause the bell tolls for thee."
2. "I can't believe that having said what I said was interpreted as having been what I said when I said it, because I said it where I said it, when I said it, and who I said it to."
3. "Martin Luther King took us to the mountaintop; I want to take us to the bank."

But as it turns out, there was a method to Ali's madness. Foreman tired, his arms dropped, and by the seventh round he ran out of steam. "I beat him for one, two, three, four rounds—beat him good," Foreman said. "At about the seventh round I had him beaten. I knew I had him. He fell on my side and whispered, 'Is that all you got, George?' I knew something strange was happening in my life because that was all I had."

For the Rope-a-Dope to work, you must allow your opponent to pummel you, you must survive said pummeling, and then, bruised and battered, you must rally to victory. It's risky, but it's the perfect strategy to apply against an opponent with superior firepower.

Similarly, in fantasy football this technique is best used when a scrappy team faces a higher-octane opponent. And it works best against a cocky, overconfident manager.

A guy like Prashun Thind.

Ah, yes, Mr. Thind. How did his week three start? Well, in the early afternoon both of his running backs ground out 100-yard days (or "hundies," as Prash calls them). Then his receivers nabbed 4 touchdowns. By the end of the four o'clock games, the Thindianapolis Colts were 50 points clear. And Thind still had his quarterback "locked and loaded" for Monday Night Football.

In short, he'd done everything he could to knock out his opponent early. Prash had thrown his haymakers. And he'd connected. Even a decent team would have succumbed to his flurry of blows.

And Thind wasn't facing a decent team. In fact, his week four opponent was quite bad, or in its "larvae stages," as its patient manager, John Schlotterbeck, suggested.

The Fat Minnesota Guys is a Rope-a-Dope team, pure and simple. While Thind started Ahman Green and the crablike Brian Westbrook, Schlots fielded Travis Minor and Tyrone Wheatley. Such a backfield would not send shivers up the spine of most fantasy managers—and indeed it didn't concern Thind, who referred to the duo as "scrub and scrubbier."

But Schlots wasn't panicked. Early in the day he merely grinned as his backs spit out 15 yards and 1 fumble, generating an underwhelming fantasy score of minus one. "That's okay," Schlots said, "The Fat Minnesota Guys are building a backfield for the future."

"But Schlots," Thind said, "you're starting Wheatley and Minor."

"So?"

"Where's the future?"

Schlots pointed at the table. "The future is . . . *right here.*"

"Where?"

"*Right here.* On my bench, learning from my starters."

Thind rolled his eyes. His lead, he felt, was insurmountable. He whispered to Kwame, "Looks like my dawgs are 2–1." Then he patted Schlots on the shoulder and added, "Winning begets more winning" before he exited the Bump-N-Run.

SIGNS YOU'RE GETTING ROPE-A-DOPED

1. Your opponent is starting a fullback and two tight ends.
2. One of your opponent's starting running backs is Mike Alstott or Zack Crockett.
3. Your opponent enters Monday Night Football with only his defense/special teams still to play.
4. Your opponent has four players involved in the Cardinals–49ers ESPN Sunday-night game.
5. Your opponent is on vacation, and has asked a fellow manager to set his lineup.

But now, as Thind gets home, he's restless. He shuttles over to his computer and rifles through porn sites. He starts with "Tantric Sex Files from the Far East," before settling on "Bollywood Babes," lured (as always) by the promise of girls who are "Hotter than red curry."

When he's done "surfing," Thind pops up his stat tracker. Like Ebenezer Scrooge counting pennies, he just wants to confirm that he's still rich. But one look at his score has him frowning.

"Ack," he says.

His team is still 20 points clear, but his lead has narrowed considerably. Worse, Schlots has somehow managed to get 15 points out of Brandon Manumaleuna and 17 points from Jay Riemersma.

"Ack," Thind says again, realizing for the first time that he hasn't quite knocked Schlots out. No, despite being an utterly crappy team, The Fat Minnesota Guys are very much alive.

Ten minutes later Prash's phone rings.

"Thind! My little friend!"

"You may dispense with the pleasantries, fat man. What do you want?"

"Good game, huh?"

"No, actually, I was destroying you."

"Still, it's exciting now, right?"

"Schlots, stop busting my balls—let me fume in peace."

"Cheer up, dude. The game's not over. You could still hold on."

"I *will* hold on."

"Okay! May the best team win."

"I *am* the best team."

"Probably . . . but on any given Sunday . . ."

"Schlots, you have absolutely no business being in this game."

"I know!"

"And you have a slim chance of winning."

"I know! Isn't that great!"

Thind hangs up, unnerved by Schlots's relentless cheeriness. Then he rechecks the score. The gap is shrinking. *Good God,* he thinks. *How humiliating. I can't possibly lose to this guy.*

Famous last words.

The Rope-a-Doper enters Monday Night Football with an improbable chance of stealing victory. In this particular case Thind has 15 points and a quarterback who averages 300 yards per game facing Schlots's . . . kicker and . . . defense.

But Schlots has him exactly where he wants him. Even Thind must admit that he's nervous, because the Rope-a-Doper always waits until the last minute before winning on a fluky touchdown or long field goal. "I've got all my ducks in a row," says Schlots, which is, in fact, true.

The tide is swinging, and Thind's arms feel as heavy as stones.

THE WILE E. COYOTE STRATEGY

Even the best-laid plans can go awry. Good managers can still start the season 0–3. All it takes is an injury, a meddlesome offensive coordinator, or an insidious burst of Mike "Skeletor" Shanahan doublespeak to change your season.

Still, starting 0–3 hurts, and hurts badly. How managers react to this adversity is a sign of their character. And usually their character is . . . strangely lacking.

Some managers panic, engineering a series of complicated trades that only succeed in making bad teams worse. Others believe that they can overcome tough starts by turning to their reserves; so they bench their struggling kicker and insert Martin "Automatica" Grammatica. Finally, certain managers take the "long view" of the season. They convince themselves that their AWOL studs will "get their numbers" over time, setting aside lingering fears that Eddie George and Stephen Davis are merely washed up.

Most 0–3 managers embrace all three views. They get involved in a series of pointless trade talks. They shuffle marginal players in and out of their starting lineups. And they wait patiently for their studs to return to form.

But these adjustments are doomed from the start. They're doomed because, at the core of things, an 0–3 manager lacks the conviction to believe in his own plans. On a rational level a savvy manager knows that it's possible to overcome this deficit. But in reality part of him already concedes that he's toast.

"Guess I shouldn't have taken Fragile Freddy this year."

"Looks like Bettis is getting the goal-line carries—damn you Duce Staley."

"Maybe Barlow *isn't* heading for a 2,000-yard season."

All lines spoken by an 0–3 manager.

Still, he must pretend that his season could turn around. This makes him seem even sadder and more frustrated than he probably is. He's like Wile E. Coyote diagramming plans to catch the Road Runner:

1. Lay on catapult.
2. Cut rope.
3. Catch Road Runner.

OR

1. Light fuse.
2. Steer Acme Rocket.
3. The Road Runner is mine.

OR

1. Carry anvil out onto tightrope.
2. Drop anvil onto Road Runner.
3. Road Runner Burger.

Wile E.'s efforts are simultaneously admirable, pathetic, and destined to fail. Such is also the case for the Bush League's own Adam Goldman, who lost by 5 points in week one, 2 points in week two, and was then crushed by Al Lopez in week three.

He didn't quit straightaway; he tried to make moves. He benched Joey Galloway, starting Jerome Pathon instead. (Galloway then proceeded to go for 120 and 2 TDs.) Now he's watching Monday Night Football, hoping against all hope that his luck will change. So he prays that his third wide receiver, who happens to be a punt returner, takes 1 back for 6.

But no. Al Michaels announces that his player is sitting out the rest of the game. Goldman's boy grins at the camera and shouts, "Never Hollywood, always neighborhood."

Goldman slams down his remote. Then he turns off his television. For a long moment he sits alone in the darkness and ponders his 0-and-3-ness. His season has spiraled beyond his control.

It's time to take a knee.

Which brings us back to Wile E. Coyote. You know what his finest moment is? It's when he is on a ledge, holding an anvil, waiting to smash the Road Runner. Then the ledge crumbles, but he stays suspended in air for a brief moment. He holds up a sign saying UH-OH! before everything slips away. His ears flutter in the wind. Sadly, and without protest, he waves to us:

Good-bye.

THE ROLLING THROUGH FALLUJAH STRATEGY

While the 0–3 manager engages in self-pity, the 3–0 manager can't contain his glee. "Well done, soldier," he says, patting himself on the back. He pops open a Bud and enjoys his victories. As a wise man once said: Mission Accomplished.

But as many great military leaders know, winning the peace is often harder than winning the war. And the 3–0 manager is now setting up shop in occupied territory. Other managers are gunning for him. There's a giant bull's-eye on his back, and there are random, turbaned fellows in dusty back-alleys hoisting Russian rocket launchers over his shoulders.

The winning manager is in a tricky situation. He still needs allies. He still needs to trade. You can't win the Bush League through sheer force alone.

Common sense dictates that you should approach conquered foes with decency, respect, and compassion. You should not, for example, blow up their camels with grenades. Nor should you crush a taxi driver's car with an M1 Abrams tank as punishment for looting plywood. And you certainly shouldn't chuckle after you've "taken out" a group of civilians.[15]

But the 3–0 manager has a hard time staying humble. He can't help it. He's won the early rounds—so why shouldn't he talk some smack? His team is the real deal, and he'll destroy anyone who questions his legitimacy. But his hubris can lead to cruel behavior.

Al Lopez is normally a decent guy. But after starting the season 3–0, he fires off e-mails declaring that his "son, Oscar, could field a better team than most Bush League managers." He ridicules Kwame, his week one victim, for his "underwhelming firepower," and Goldman, his week three opponent, for "folding faster than a Chinese Laundromat."

---

15. The Fallujah "Take 'Em Out" air-strike video stands out as the grimmest moment of the Iraq War. A fighter pilot sees a group of guys in white cloaks scuttling down an alley. He says to HQ: "I got a big . . . group of people. . . . Should I take them out?" Without hesitation HQ replies: "Take 'em out." A moment later the group on the ground explodes in a ball of flames, and the pilot says, "Awww, dude." Like a stoner watching fireworks.

Worse still, Al uses his early strength as leverage, making stiff trade demands. He dismisses The Mick, who needs a backup tight end, because he sees "nothing that the Irish Potato Famine can offer—absolutely nothing."

"Dude, it's a long season," The Mick says. "Chill out."

"I'm sorry. I just love my team."

"Yeah, but you're acting like there's no way your team can be improved. Like you don't need any trading partners."

"Honestly, I don't. I'm looking at my team, and I don't see any holes."

"Long season, Al. Long season."

Al won't be a coalition builder. He has insulted allies with whom he's worked closely in the past. That has annoyed the Bush League. Now e-mails are circulating about *getting Al Lopez's black-beaned Calle Ocho ass.*

So yes, it's true—Al Lopez has lit up his first three opponents. He's rolled into Fallujah, flags-a-fluttering. He's done his victory dance. But he's also stirred up a group of insurgents. And as Lopez falls asleep, happy with his 3-and-0-ness, a scrappy group of rebels are already huddled together, planning their counterstrike.

THE RUBIK'S CUBE STRATEGY

The 2–1 managers are the hardest to understand. Is the glass half-full or half-empty?

For the optimistic manager a 2–1 start presents a kind of puzzle. Yes, his team has flaws. Yes, he needs to be very careful with trades. But perhaps—*perhaps*—with just a few tweaks, everything will fall into place, and a play-off run will still be possible.

He's like a twelve-year-old trying to solve Rubik's Cube. So far he's managed to get two faces done, but the other sides are all jumbled. And every time he turns a section, his situation only becomes more confusing.

Still, at least there's hope. Many champions have shaken off early season losses to win a league. The campaign has just started.

We can't say the same thing for 4–4 or 5–5 managers. By midseason, perceptions are pretty much set. It doesn't matter if a manager has been "competitive" in most games. These teams simply aren't going anywhere.

They're the Al Gores of fantasy football. They came *this close* to being a legitimate threat. But then they fumbled some dimpled chads in Florida and lost a tight game they had to win. Now all that's left is to grow a beard, add a paunch, and start an ill-defined cable channel.

GORE-ISMS

1. "When my sister and I were growing up, there was never any doubt in our minds that men and women were equal, if not more so."
2. "We are ready for any unforeseen event that may or may not occur."
3. "I believe we are on an irreversible trend toward more freedom and democracy—but that could change."

Kwame Jones is 2–1. He likes his team but knows that problems must be addressed. Yes, his one loss was fluky, but he can't go 2–2 or 3–3. That will not do.

So Kwame trolls the free-agent market, hoping to make subtle but important upgrades. He spends sixty free-agent dollars on David Terrell, a wide receiver who "went off" for 126 yards on 3 catches against the Detroit Lions. After picking him up, Kwame sends a note to Lopez saying that at this rate *"Terrell will have an 1,800-yard season."*

El Matador responds: *"And Jesus will come back from the dead for goal-line carries, earning 14 TDs on 17 carries."*

Kwame smiles. He smiles because Lopez doesn't understand. No one in the Bush League understands—not yet, not really. They don't get that Kwame has been working on his team, molding it into place. And with just one more turn, maybe, just maybe, everything will finally come together.

THE GOLLUM STRATEGY

The converse of the optimistic 2–1 manager is the grumpy 1–2 manager. The guy who looks for excuses. Who believes he's been screwed. Who refuses to accept that his team is mediocre.

After starting the season 0–2 and then narrowly avoiding an 0–3 start during a low-scoring Week Three win, Chris O'Brien claims that his team is "the unluckiest of the unlucky." He believes that Bush League managers are conspiring against him, that there's something wrong with the league scoring system, that the free-agent market is fixed.

His rantings are Nixonian in both style and substance.[16] So long as he's winning, O'Brien is calm and coolheaded. But hang two losses on him and he'll start bitching about how everything is stacked against him.

NIXON-ISMS

1. "I would have made a good pope."
2. "Get a good night's sleep, and don't bug anybody without asking me."
3. "I gave 'em a sword. And they stuck it in, and they twisted it with relish. And I guess if I had been in their position, I'd have done the same thing."

---

16. To put Nixon's paranoia in perspective, consider the people who were on his "enemies list" as of 1970: Joe Namath, Gregory Peck, Steve McQueen, and the always pesky Judith Martin (aka "Miss Manners").

Which brings us to his strategy. You could finesse it, you could sugarcoat it, you could try to explain it a number of different ways. But at the end of the day, when O'Brien goes 1–2, he pretty much starts rooting for injuries.

The logic behind this decision is murky at best. If his team is doing poorly, he tries to "equalize" by hoping that other teams will suck too. Or, as Schlots puts it, "The Mick worships at the shrine of schadenfreude."

The Mick's occultism has a history. Several years ago Schlots was having a solid year, rolling behind Fred Taylor, when he started making comments about "riding his FT horse to fantasy football glory." This infuriated O'Brien. So one afternoon in the Bump-N-Run, The Mick closed his eyes, prayed for Taylor to have a season-ending knee injury, and when he looked up, a stretcher was carting Fragile Freddy off the field.

The Mick felt imbued with magical powers.

Over subsequent seasons he wished ill on as many players as possible. Often his prayers were answered. We think this is simply because football is a violent sport. But The Mick claims that he has a gift for "channeling" injuries.

"I bring the fury. I bring the pain," says O'Brien.

He is a fantasy football black magician. But such a practice is not without its problems. For one thing, karma can be a bitch: The Irish Potato Famine has been the most banged-up team in Bush League history.

Last year, in consecutive weeks, O'Brien's starting running back, quarterback, and wide receiver all suffered season-ending injuries.

Bam, bam, bam. Just like that. Old Western–style.

"Oh, great," The Mick said. "Could I get screwed any harder?" He smiled ironically to himself, and then he closed his eyes and prayed for more injuries.

The Mick is like Gollum after he became addicted to the Ring. At one point his use of dark magic was probably interesting. But then he took it too far, turned all radioactive and Sam Cassell–like, and spent the remaining eleven hundred pages of Tolkien's epic droning on and on about his "precious" and "sneaky little hobbitses—wicked, tricksy, false!"

Fear The Mick and his curses.

After his team's 1–2 start, it's the smart play.

ON PREDICTING INJURIES

According to a variety of Web sites, you can predict injuries by looking at "durability factors." For example, a player who started fourteen or more games the previous season and was never listed as "doubtful" or "probable" will show up as "questionable" or "doubtful" 61 percent less often than the average player the following season. (For more info, check out 4for4.com.)

11

<< I AM GRIFFIN, >>
HEAR ME ROAR

AMONG THE MANY BUSH LEAGUE TRADITIONS, NONE IS more absurd than The Griffin Ceremony, which has been invoked twice over the league's eight-year history.

The mechanics behind the ritual are simple: If any manager starts the season 0–4, he must wear Thind's sacred Griffin Suit, which Thind stole from his old high school, for a night out on the town. Refusal to comply leads to a suspension (which happened once, to Owen Greavy, manager of the Motor City Rumblers, in 1998—his team had an often mocked and never repeated Tony Richardson/Fred Beasley backfield).

Tonight members of the Bush League are meeting at the Bump-N-Run to initiate a new member into the brotherhood of Griffins: The Bitter Drafter.

"Bitter Drafter," Thind says. "We need to talk logistics. It's Griffin time."

"Buzz off, Thind. I'm not interested."

"You have no choice. It's Bush League tradition. You know the deal. If you don't oblige, you're out of the league. And you don't want to give all the guys in this league who hate you that satisfaction, do you?"

"You're right. I can't have that."

"Now you're talking."

"Why are you in charge of this?"

"I'm the Bush League scribe. This is my domain."

"Figures. So what do I have to do?"

"Well, our league constitution states that an 0–4 manager must wear the traditional Griffin costume to a bar and hit the dance floor. And when I say 'dance,' I mean really dance. Further, if someone asks you who you are, you must respond, 'I am Griffin, hear me roar!'"

"That's the deal?"

"That's the deal."

"Anything else?"

"One other thing: If anyone asks you what a griffin is, you must answer that a griffin is a mythical creature with the head of an eagle and the body of a lion."

"I see. And if I tell you to go screw yourself?"

"You're out."

"Can't have that."

"No. Can't have that."

"Damn it."

"Here's the costume. Put it on."

Thind hands The Bitter Drafter a furry Griffin costume. The Griffin features an eagle head, complete with yellow beak, and a brown shaggy lion's body. A long ratty tail is attached to the back.

The Bitter Drafter grudgingly slips it on.

Thind remains deadly serious.

"It's hot as Laguna Beach in here."

"Yes, it's rather toasty, isn't it?"

"Have you worn this thing?"

"Don't be ridiculous."

"God! It's itchy as hell."

"Yep."

"And scratchy."

"Yep."

"Dude, I can't see out of the eyeholes."

"Right. Watch your step."

Thind and The Bitter Drafter enter the bar. The Mick, Kwame, and Goldman emerge from the shadows. Kwame pats The Bitter Drafter's eagle head, and Goldman shakes his enormous furry paw. "It's go time," Thind says. "Do the hustle, baby."

The Mick pushes The Bitter Drafter onto the dance floor. He trudges out to the center, raising and lowering his cumbersome mascot feet. He looks back at the guys to see if they're serious, and they each give him a thumbs-up. The Griffin's tail drags several feet behind him.

The Griffin begins dancing by himself. He sways his hips back and forth, and swings his arms wildly. He periodically looks back at the other Bush Leaguers, who are now laughing hysterically. He stops moving his feet, but the guys motion for him to continue. Begrudgingly he resumes dancing.

Three minutes into his routine a woman approaches.

"What's with the costume?"

"Um, uh, well, I am Griffin, hear me roar."

"Huh?"

"I am Griffin, hear me roar!"

"Well, let's hear it. Roar."

"Roar. Um, let me try that again. Roarrrrr!"

"Not much of a roar."

"Yeah, well."

During this conversation the Griffin has lost track of his tail. His herky-jerky dancing dragged it through a puddle of spilled beer, and now there's an oafish guy standing on it. The Griffin bends over and tugs at the tail, freeing it from the guy's heel.

He stands back up. The woman hasn't left.

"What the hell is a griffin anyway?"

"A griffin is, uh, a mythical creature with the head of an eagle and the body of a lion."

"Do all Griffins hold their tails in their paws?"

"Only when it's getting dragged through beer."

"So why are you roaring? Shouldn't you be screeching? Like an eagle?"

"I hadn't really given it much thought."

"Maybe you should consider it."

"Fair point. 'Screech.'"

"Is that your best screech?"

"Screech! Screech!"

"Excuse me, miss," Thind says, stepping between them. "Is the Griffin giving you any trouble?"

"Man, you all are fools. But I dig the costume."

"Screech."

"Dude, it's 'Roar!' What's with the 'Screech'? Don't mess around, bro. Don't tempt fate."

"Sorry," The Bitter Drafter says. "Um, uh, roarrrrr."

"That's better. Much better. Now break it down, Griffin. Break. It. Down."

12

<< THE ART OF THE DEAL >>

"An object in possession seldom retains the same charm
that it had in pursuit."—Pliny the Younger

SINCE THE DAWN OF TIME MAN HAS TRADED. PREHISTORIC
cavemen swapped sticks for stones, animal skins for animal meat, and
women for women. With the emergence of ancient civilizations, man
began exchanging land. Or conquering it, as the case may be. In
today's modern age anything can be traded—shares of stock, MP3s, or
even gerrymandered congressional districts.[17]

Trading generally involves exchanging possessions of equal value.
You give and you get. Everyone benefits. That's the theory anyway.
But inevitably there's a winner and a loser. And the worse the loser's
trade, the more interesting the result becomes.

Throughout history there have been pathetic trades. In 1625, the
Canarsee Delaware tribe exchanged the rights to Manhattan with the
Dutch for twenty-four dollars worth of beads. In today's dollars, that's
the equivalent of a Duran Duran double-box set. That's a pathetic
trade—even if the South Street Seaport still smells fishy.

In the sports world, Boston sent Babe Ruth to New York for a
hundred thousand dollars, cursing the Red Sox for decades. It took a

---

17. Massachusetts governor Elbridge Gerry, who crafted a district for political purposes that looked like
a salamander, created the original gerrymander in 1812. We mention this primarily because we find
salamanders to be cute albeit slippery creatures.

modern-day choke job by Mariano Rivera and the rest of the Yankees to reverse said curse. Yet, still a pathetic trade.

MOST-LOPSIDED TRADES IN SPORTS HISTORY

1. Red Sox trade Babe Ruth to the Yankees for cash.
2. Minnesota gets Herschel Walker for a bushel of draft picks; builds the Cowboys dynasty.
3. Golden State trades Robert Parish and the number-three pick (which is used on Kevin McHale) to Boston for the number-one pick, which is used on Joe Barry Carroll.
4. Atlanta trades Brett Favre to Green Bay for what later becomes RB Tony Smith and CB Frankie Smith.
5. Milwaukee Bucks trade Lew Alcindor to the LA Lakers for a few scrubs and old *Laverne & Shirley* tapes.

It's no different in fantasy football. Given the right circumstances, managers have swapped Terrell Owens for Stacey Mack. Or Donovan McNabb for Zack Crockett. These trades appear preposterous at first glance. But they happen.

And how, exactly, do they happen? Napoléon Bonaparte, a diminutive man who won his share of big battles, said, "Never interrupt your enemy when he is making a mistake." One party simply flailed. Fell asleep at the switch.

But it's not just the losing trade partner who's negatively impacted. Quite the contrary. A trade ripples across the fantasy football landscape, impacting other parties, shifting the balance of power, and ultimately altering the competitive terrain.

After all, the notion of win-win is so five minutes ago.

BLOOD IN THE WATER

The likely first trade of the season—the shark and guppy trade—pairs the most experienced fantasy manager with the least. But this isn't really a trade; it's a massacre.

A guppy, as far as fantasy football is concerned, is an inexperienced manager. Someone vulnerable to a lopsided trade. Someone waiting to be outfoxed. Or someone who's just dopey and prone to dumping good players.

The guppy is like former Iraqi Information Minister Baghdad Bob. He's totally out of touch with reality, and unaware or unwilling to admit that the American forces are a mere mile outside the city. All the while, he's surrounded, his fate sealed.

BAGHDAD BOB–ISMS

1. "We have destroyed two tanks, fighter planes, two helicopters, and their shovels."
2. "Britain is not worth an old shoe."
3. "We will push those crooks, those mercenaries, back into the swamp."

In the Bush League The Two-Headed Hydra is the prototypical guppy squad. They had a lousy draft, their team is struggling, and now their players are chum—oily bits of fish ground up and scattered in the water.

The shark, by contrast, is a fierce competitor. A ravenous hunter who won't tire until he's found his prey. Thind, Schlots, Lopez, and The Mick are all sharks. Or at least they all consider themselves sharks. Up until the moment the rug is pulled out from beneath them and they, too, are revealed to be guppylike.

But that's a separate discussion.

Ocean-dwelling sharks are known for their highly refined sense of smell and their heightened ability to sense from miles away even the slightest motions in the water. The sharks of the Bush League likewise can smell guppy blood in the water. And when they do, they hurtle themselves like sleek torpedoes toward the awaiting prey.

Once they've arrived, they cut a series of ever tightening circles, their dorsal fins barely breaking the surface.

"Hydra," O'Brien says, "tough start to the season. Perhaps we could exchange some players to bolster your lineup."

"Hydra," Lopez says, "help me help you."

"Hydra," Thind says, "let's cut to the chase: Kindly hand over your players. Now."

If the guppy says, "We're holding tight," the circling continues.

But if the guppy responds, "Our squad has not come together as we'd hoped—we're open to discussing anything," the sharks move in for the kill.

When it's time for a final strike, the most aggressive shark approaches a guppy much in the way Scorpion from Mortal Kombat would assail a weakened foe. He slings his supernatural bullwhip, catches his prey around the neck, and pulls him close with a ghoulish "Get over here!" The unsuspecting and dazed guppy, listing on rubber legs, wobbles in front of his opponent, awaiting his coup de grace.

And when the übershark strikes successfully, outmaneuvering all the other sharks, the thrashing of The Hydra can be felt from a great distance. The guppy may not know it yet, but he just had a chunk of flesh torn from his already weakened fantasy roster.

Such is the case when Schlots moves Moe Williams and Onterrio Smith for Terrell Owens. The trade ripples across the Bush League, and the other sharks are none too pleased. They missed their meal, and someone else just got a protein infusion.

"Two-Headed Hydra, you absolute amateurs!" gasps Thind. "I can't believe you agreed to that trade. I would have given you much,

much more for TO. You've upset the entire balance of the Bush League. Why on earth would you agree to that?"

Hydra, still in shock from the attack and only now registering the true damage that's been done, is left meekly explaining: "We needed to shake things up, and now we've cornered the Minnesota running game."

Somewhere in the depths of the Bush League, the winning shark smiles a toothy smile, swallows once, and swims on.

THE KABUKI DANCE

In trade talks involving experienced managers, negotiations are much more sophisticated. Stalemates are far more common. Thus, trade discussions take on an added level of importance.

Mark Twain once said, "The rule is perfect: in all matters of opinion our adversaries are insane." This is a key concept to the underlying notion of trading in fantasy football. Whatever your trading partner is offering, it's certainly too little. Whatever they're asking, it's unquestionably too much.

The language of trading becomes as important as the players involved. One must poke and prod, jib and jab, parry and strike.

First you must express a false interest in your fellow manager's life—the implication being that you're just "checking in" and having a "friendly chat."

The second step is to compliment your trade partner's players. The key here is to heap false praise on players in which you have no interest while avoiding mention of the players that you covet.

Even though The Mick is 1–3 and Lopez is 3–1, they still need to engage in these rituals. Each season Al Lopez and The Mick enter heated trade discussions. In every instance known to the Bush League, they have failed to execute a trade. The chemistry just isn't right. But like Bighorn Rams they size each other up, slam heads a few times, and then trot off to chew on some grass.

True to form, the language is always the same: seemingly well conceived, initially neutral in tone, and always laden with falsehoods and misdirection.

"O'Brien, it's Al. How's it going?" Lopez says.

"You know. The usual. Same junky job, same junky office."

"Right on."

"So, how's your wife and daughter?"

"You mean Oscar, my son?

"Right. Yeah, your son. I meant to say 'son.'"

"They're both great. Just great. Vanessa is a constant thorn in my side, but that's her job. I deserve it, usually. And Oscar's a real handful these days. But it's all worth it. Fatherhood is a special experience. I never expected to be so into it."

"I can imagine. Well, I guess I can't. But that's great. Glad to hear it."

"Yup."

"Cool."

"Cool."

There's an uncomfortable silence. It's time to shift gears. "Dude," Lopez says, "you had a nice, nice draft, by the way. Snagging Donald Driver in the seventh round was tight. You got some solid depth at the wide receiver position."

"Thanks, man."

"Sure, no problem."

"So, let's cut to the chase."

"Yes, let's."

"What do you want?"

The two men begin to circle each other.

Lopez states, "Can we stipulate first that I'm annoyed that you took Willis McGahee? Travis Henry's my starting running back, and I wanted him handcuffed. McGahee means more to me than he does to you. Besides, his value will plummet after Henry inevitably reels off three solid games in a row."

The Mick doesn't respond. He's waiting to see where Al is going.

"Let's make something happen here before we get burdened by shifting player value," says Lopez. "May I humbly suggest: Eddie Kennison for Willis McGahee.

"The rationale here," Lopez continues, not letting O'Brien speak, "is that you won't start McGahee at all, and I'd argue that Eddie Kennison, who's the number-one wide receiver on an extremely potent Chiefs offense, would start for you as a third wide receiver."

"El Matador, thanks," replies O'Brien. "Seriously, I didn't even know you had Henry when I drafted McGahee. I was just looking at the board and took him based on talent. I think he's sweet, was sweet at Miami, and so on.

"A fairer trade," he continues, "would be to move Warrick Dunn for McGahee. That way you'd wrap up Buffalo's running game and I'd nail down Atlanta's. Dunn has more value now, but will likely be in a running-back-by-committee with T. J. Duckett for the year even if he's healthy.[18] Thoughts on this?"

This response is met by silence as well.

"O'Brien, thank you for your counteroffer—"

"No problem—"

"But that is . . ." Lopez is searching for the right conciliatory phrase. "That is . . . absolutely fucking preposterous. You're asking for a starting running back for one that may never get off the bench."

Swiftly, suddenly, acrimony enters the conversation.

"What do you mean preposterous? You're offering me Eddie Kennison—a rather dodgy, toadlike, grumpy guy who quit on a former team and never caught more than 1,000 yards in a season. You're literally offering me mediocrity. The Mick doesn't stand for mediocrity."

"Yes," Lopez says, his throat tightening, "we all appreciate your winning tradition, as well as your four straight seasons of sub .500 ball—"

---

18. T. J. Duckett is probably the most frequently bandied-about name in shark-to-shark trades that are never consummated.

"That ended two years ago—"

"Nevertheless, we're talking about a starting number-two wide receiver versus a number-four running back who's sitting on your bench. I'm offering you immediate value. I'm offering you a player that starts for your team tomorrow."

"Ah yes, the old value argument. Well, yes, you *might* be offering me more immediate value. But I'm a long-term-growth guy."

"Oh, no, please don't use that phrase—"

"Seriously, Kennison is a one-week fix. Average. Uninspiring. And again, toadlike in appearance. On the other hand McGahee has massive upside. I have him projected to beat out Henry by week three—"

"You have, um, backup running back *projections?*"

"Yes, I most certainly do. I have Willis projected to beat him out by—"

"Beat him out! Are you joking?"

"No," O'Brien says. "My projections are not jokes."

"Henry is an All-Pro. McGahee is recovering from a torn ACL."

"Yes, but The Mick likes his burstability."

"His what?"

"His burstability. McGahee has great burstability. Kwame was the first guy to tout his burstability, and I agree. Which is why The Mick drafted him. He could go on to be one of the best running backs in the game. And The Mick is all about finding greatness."

"O'Brien, if you speak one more time in the third person, this conversation is over. You're not Deion Sanders. Stop speaking in the third person."

"Well, you're throwing me an insulting offer. You're offering me a Nissan Maxima with fifty thousand miles in exchange for a Maserati that's still sitting in the showroom. It makes no sense."

Lopez sighs in frustration. "I can just imagine you cackling like Gargamel over his cauldron, ready to boil some Smurfs. You must be so proud. But for the life of me, I have no idea what you're actually saying."

TOP SMURFS

1. **Clumsy Smurf.** Wears baggy cap, collects rocks.
2. **Finance Smurf.** Introduced gold-coined money system to Smurf-land.
3. **Grandpa Smurf.** Favorite expression: "Smurfatoodles!"
4. **Scaredy Smurf.** Liked by Smurfette because he's more "sensitive" than the other guys.
5. **Weakling Smurf.** Used performance-enhancing drugs to win the Smurf Olympics.

"And you're speaking in your standard form of gibberish when you compare relative values of wide receivers and running backs," O'Brien says. "I'm a simple man, with simple tastes. Why would I do that trade? Why would *The Mick* do that trade?"

"O'Brien, you're infuriating me. I'm infuriated."

"Well, The Mick's not thrilled either."

"Let's bottom-line this: What in your opinion is a fair—and I repeat *fair*—offer for McGahee."

O'Brien pauses for a moment. He hems. He haws. "The Mick thinks, honestly, that either Warrick Dunn, Travis Henry, or both represents fair trade value."

"That's it, we're done here," Lopez snaps. "O'Brien, you strike me as a bad guy. Not a bad-intentioned guy. So I know you're not intentionally trying to enrage me. You're just a guy who happens to be bad. Innately. I'm not sure which is worse, but I do know that speaking to you for more than five minutes makes my skin crawl."

"What can I say?" The Mick says, chuckling.

"You can say whatever you want. I'm never dealing with you again. I have too much going on to get bogged down with you. You're not logical. You're not even *rational*. And I don't imagine I will speak to you ever again about a trade. Ever. *Vaya con Dios*."

With that, Lopez hangs up, shaking his head in disgust.

"*Adiós, muchacho,*" O'Brien says to the empty phone. He stares straight ahead, absently chewing his lip, remaining otherwise motionless.

This trade, suffice it to say, is never consummated. It is the epitome of a nontrade trade. In fact, Lopez and O'Brien were merely engaged in a well-choreographed routine. A dance they do every year. A dance that had them waving their hands in the air, sighing repeatedly, and engaging in assorted other histrionics.

So the two shuffle off, ready to begin rummaging through other guys' lineups, their Kabuki dance concluded. For the moment.

REARRANGING THE DECK CHAIRS ON THE *TITANIC*

Heading into week five, Goldman is operating on borrowed time. He's got to make a move, and soon, or his season will be lost. He'll have nothing to play for and will be left fending off his fiancée with "just one more minute" responses.

Initially Goldman launches aggressive trade talks. He lobs a few calls in to Kwame. He's looking for a stud running back and asks for Priest Holmes, but Kwame tells him that he's untradable.[19] Goldman then sidles up to Lopez. But again, Lopez is asking for some serious value in return.

So Goldman settles on his trademark move: He does some minor lineup tweaking. He returns to Kwame—a reliable guy. They banter back and forth, tossing around various uninspiring names. Quickly they eliminate the majority of choices, leaving only a few scraps.

"Adam, just do something," Kwame says. "You need to revamp your entire backfield. Propose something, anything. And I can probably move one of my quarterbacks."

"I have nothing to offer other than two decent tight ends," Goldman laments. "I may just sit back."

---

19. Of course Kwame is right to keep Holmes on ice, but nothing destroys the trade fabric of a league faster than designating a stud RB "untradable." Without workhorses you're left with tight end for tight end trades or, worse, the dreaded wide-receiver-for-free-agent-dollars swap.

"Ouch. Give my best to Jay Fiedler."

Finally Goldman relents. He's tired of this, exhausted by the inanity of it all. What, really, is the point? "Fine. How about Bubba Franks for Drew Bledsoe? I could do that."

Kwame shrugs. "I suppose I could use Bubba."

"All right, done."

There it is. Goldman consummates his first trade of the season. And what a snoozer it is. Drew Bledsoe for Bubba Franks. Two utterly forgettable fantasy players. The ultimate low-impact trade.

Kicking the proverbial can down the proverbial road.

"Congratulations, Adam," says Kwame. "You've shaken up your team. This should really turn things around."

"Yeah, well."

Goldman knows that little has been accomplished, but at least he did something. Nevertheless, the Team Goyim ship continues to take on water.

Goldman's merely rearranging the deck chairs on the *Titanic*. The layout might be different, but the results will still be the same. This trade has changed nothing. He's sinking, and faster than he'd care to admit.

TWO OF SHIT IS STILL SHIT

In real life a team that trades many players for one guy is usually getting jacked—look at gimpy Herschel Walker going to the Vikings for something like twenty-eight players, a few cars, a ball boy, and a Hubert Humphrey autograph. Or witness the Saints giving up a bunch of draft picks for Ricky Williams, a batch of dreadlocks, and a picture of then-coach Ditka posing with a man in a wedding dress.

But fantasy football is entirely different. A savvy manager wants to dislodge "studs," and he can sometimes achieve that by dangling a motley crew of characters to a manager who caves just because "it's too damn confusing to sort through all the stats and adjusted lineups."

In the Bush League the Merlinesque Prashun Thind is the master of this trade strategy. Typically he starts by whipping up an Excel model that analyzes "trailing average" stats over the past four weeks and "going forward" projections. No one understands what any of this means. But it must mean something. Because it's in a spreadsheet.

With printouts in tow Thind edges up to his prey, an unwitting guppy. "Hey, I noticed you have several holes in your lineup. I thought that I might be able to offer some depth."

"Um, yeah, it's been a tough season so far. I don't even know where to start. I got problems at quarterback and wide receiver."

"Perhaps I can interest you in a package deal. I give you some of my depth, you get several players you can start immediately, and you ship me, I don't know, say, Corey Dillon."

"Hmm, that seems like a lot to ask for."

"To get, you gotta give."

The guppy knows he's in trouble. He tries a little self-deprecating humor to ward off the shark's advances. "Well, as the Arizona Cardinals of the Bush League, I'm just praying that none of my players will get their necks broken this weekend."

Thind is undaunted.

"You need immediate help. You need guys you can start. In short: my guys. I propose sending you three starters for just one of yours. So how about: Steve McNair, Donte Stallworth, and Mike Andersen for Corey Dillon?"

This is a preposterous trade offer, but one that the guppy has to consider. He could, in fact, start all three of Thind's players.

"Let me think about it."

This scenario calls to mind the great words of Dennis Miller. And when we say great words, we refer to the old-school Dennis Miller.[20] This is in contrast to the new-school Dennis Miller, who busies himself shilling for NetZero.

Anyhow, Miller once said, "Two of shit is still shit." And that's the

---

20. We actually think Miller, like many comedians, is at his best when he's tripping and stumbling. He's less smirky. One gem from his fleeting work on Monday Night Football: "That kid's got an arm like Uncle Fester at an exhibition of pre-Columbian . . . um, Christ, I lost it. I was going for something thick. So what's with the beard, Grizzly Fouts?"

essence of Thind's multiplayer trade offers. Thind showers his prey with shit. Useless stones for his prey's gold.

And sometimes it works.

Advantage, Thind.

PLAYERS COMMONLY INVOLVED IN PACKAGE DEALS

We can't confirm this, but league sources tell us that Donte' Stallworth has been involved in almost every miscellaneous package-deal over the last three years. Other package-deal players include:

1. David Patten
2. Michael Pittman
3. Brian Griese
4. Ernie Conwell
5. Az-Zahir Hakim

NO SOUP FOR YOU— THE DEAD-BEFORE-IT-STARTS TRADE

Some guys simply won't trade. With anyone. Ever.

This manager is viewed with detached frustration by the rest of the league. "He's a cost of doing business," Lopez says. "A ghost in the machine," Goldman notes. But despite their best efforts to "live with" the problem, the Guy Who Won't Trade is a roadblock. He can't help others, and he certainly can't help himself—even if his team is hurtling toward an 0–6 start.

There are a variety of reasons why a manager won't trade. Perhaps he can't find fair offers. Perhaps the entire league is thin at the position he needs most. Or perhaps he's simply too attached to his players. But even the most loyal manager must have trade bait. Say, a husky Ron Dayne or a tipsy Kerry Collins.

Unless, of course, that guy is The Bitter Drafter. He's the Soup Nazi of trading. He'd rather decline opportunities than compromise his convictions. What his convictions are, exactly, remain unclear.

Perhaps more than anything he's someone who simply enjoys saying no.

The only thing that's more amazing than this guy returning to the Bush League year after year, wreaking his own brand of stubborn havoc, is that another league member, despite all evidence to the contrary, will still initiate trade discussions with him.

"Hey, man. Schlots here."

"Schlots, how's it going? You still chubby?"

"What? Oh, um, yeah I guess I'm still chubby."

"Great to hear. Eat like the wind. So, what do you want?"

"Well, I was just looking at your lineup, and it seems the injury bug has bitten you. Looks like you could use some help at running back. I got some depth there, and could use one of your wide receivers."

"Yeah, I'm not interested."

"Wait, I haven't even told you which player I'm offering."

"Yeah, I'm not interested."

"Hold on a sec—"

"Yeah. I'm not interested."

"Let me explain—"

"Not. Interested."

Schlots, befuddled, hangs up the phone and rubs the back of his neck. That charm offensive didn't even get off the runway. Such a scenario calls to mind George Costanza's dealings with the notorious Soup Nazi on *Seinfeld*.

George Costanza: Um, excuse me. I—I think you forgot my bread.
Soup Nazi: Bread: two dollars extra.

George Costanza: Two dollars? But everyone in front of me got free bread.

Soup Nazi: You want bread?

George Costanza: Yes, please.

Soup Nazi: Three dollars!

George Costanza: What?

Soup Nazi: No soup for you! [*The Soup Nazi snaps his fingers; the cashier takes George's soup and returns his money.*]

The Bitter Drafter is having none of it and wishes to be left alone. His team will remain his team, and no one can convince him otherwise.

OTHER TRADES

1. **The Fire Sale**: The guy who moves every starter off his team
2. **The Player for Free-Agent Dollars Trade:** Collusion usually involved
3. **The "Sell High" Trade:** Manager moves wide receiver off team after monster week never to be repeated again
4. **The "Iron Curtain" Trade:** Trade between managers who work together and won't trade with anyone else in the league, perfected by the Bush League's own "Merrill Lynch Mafia" between 1994 and 2000.
5. **The Handcuff Trade:** Manager overpays to get his stud's backup
6. **The Iran-Contra Trade:** Talent or resources filtered from superpower team to guerilla insurgent team for politically motivated reasons
7. **The Special-Teams Trade:** No comment
8. **The Injured Player Trade:** Unwitting move for a guy who's dinged up
9. **The Multiteam Trade:** Junk for junk for junk
10. **The Reverse Fleece Trade:** A trade that has managers up in arms over how one guy's getting fleeced; at the end of the season it's discovered that the reverse has actually occurred

13

<< A LIVING WILL AND >>
THE MIAMI DOLPHINS

LOPEZ SETTLES INTO HIS COUCH. HE GRABS SOME DORITOS and pops open a Sam Adams. Then he dials The Mick. He doesn't enjoy chatting with The Mick, but because the two are in the same division, he feels an obligation to talk shop.

"How do you feel about your matchup with Goldman this week?" Al asks.

"Well, I'm thinking about turning Clintonious Portisus loose."

"His name is Clinton Portis."

"Right . . ."

"Don't call him Clintonious Portisus. He's not a Roman senator."

"Whatever, compadre. It's going to be smooth sailing."

Vanessa enters the living room and sits down next to Al. She doesn't love the NFL, but usually commits to watching at least a half with her husband.

"All right, O'Brien, I'm out. Vanessa's here."

"Say hi to her for me."

Turning to Vanessa, Al says, "Chris O'Brien says hi."

Vanessa nods gently and flips through *In Touch Weekly*.

Al hangs up the phone, leans back, and puts his arm around Vanessa.

"I hate that guy," she says.

"Why is that?"

"He's a sneaky little know-it-all." Vanessa hasn't spent more than an hour with the Bush Leaguers, but she has steadfast opinions on all of them. Two years ago The Mick called at the wrong time, then chuckled in the wrong way about "fleecing" her husband on a trade, and that was that.

Vanessa puts her head in Al's lap and kicks her legs onto the couch. Al places his beer on her shoulder for easier access. Vanessa nibbles on an occasional chip, swearing that each one will be her last.

The Redskins-Browns game kicks off. The Browns quickly go three-and-out and punt to the Redskins. Al is riveted.

"Alejandro, I want to talk to you about something."

"Busy, baby, busy."

"This is important—hear me out. I think we need a living will."

"Uh-huh."

"I want you to know that if I get in some terrible accident and I'm all hooked up with tubes, you should pull the plug. I don't want any of that."

Al leans forward, hoping that Vanessa will talk herself out.

"Honey, I'm serious. This is important. Not just for me but for Oscar, too."

"Sure, baby, I hear you." Portis charges through the Browns defensive line (if it can be called "defensive," or even a "line"), gobbling up yards. "My God! You could drive an eighteen-wheeler through that hole!"

Vanessa persists. "Alejandro, if you were on life support, I'd want to pull the plug. I couldn't stand to see you go through that. And I don't think you'd want that, right?"

At the mention of his wife's prematurely ending Al's life, Portis pounds into the end zone. Al sighs. Stares stone-faced.

"Vanessa, you're killing me. Sorry, that's a poor choice of words. But come on. You see me watching this game. You know *all* I want to do is watch *this* game. I can't focus on what you're asking me."

Vanessa shakes her head. "I wish you would place greater importance on serious matters of life and death than watching a crappy football game."

Al *is* thinking about it, though. He's trying not to, but he can't avoid it. "Vanessa, I think we should get our wills done, okay? But in the meantime, if the Browns keep choking on offense, Portis will get his obligatory 120 yards and 2 touches, and the division will go to Chris O'Brien. I will lose out on two hundred and fifty dollars. And we can't have that, can we?"

Vanessa crinkles her eyes. Al has a point. She looks at the television. The anemic Browns' offense takes the field. "Who's the quarterback?"

"Jeff Garcia."

"Who is he?"

"He went to San Jose State. Terrell Owens claimed he was gay."

"So what does it matter *if* he's gay?"

"It doesn't matter, Vanessa. Nothing TO says matters. And he's known to date women anyway."

"C'mon, Garcia," Vanessa shouts. "Throw the ball down the field for the rest of the period."

"It's quarter."

"What?"

"Football has four quarters."

"Whatever," Vanessa says. "Just win the thing."

<< THE "WHO DO I START?" >>
FOG OF WAR DIALOGUE

THE FOLLOWING E-MAIL EXCHANGE TAKES PLACE BETWEEN Prashun Thind and Al Lopez. Prashun has two viable running backs in Ahman Green and Curtis Martin. But he can start only one. Thind is asking Lopez for his advice, even though it's unclear whether Lopez is offering credible insight or pure misdirection.

From: Thind, Prashun
Sent: Tuesday, November 9, 2004 9:53 PM
To: Alejandro Lopez
Subject: Opinion Needed

Need a recommendation on whether to start Curtis Martin this weekend v. *your* Miami Dolphins.

Should I pass on him against MIA's run defense? I could go with Ahman Green v. the Redskins instead. But I hate Martin.

Talk to me.

From: Lopez, Alejandro
Sent: Tuesday, November 9, 2004 10:01 PM
To: Prashun Thind
Subject: Re: Opinion Needed

Tough one . . . I think you're supposed to go with your stud, i.e., Ahman Green. You can't back off the guy just because he's going against a good D.

On the other hand Martin is a faux-stud too. And although it pains me to say it, he could run wild against my Dolphins. (Bowens is older and Ogunleye, who left as a free agent, played the run very, very well. They haven't found adequate replacements.)

If anything, I think our sputtering (initially, anyway) offense will give Martin plenty of chances to be on the field.

On the other hand Ahman Green is Ahman Green.

From: Thind, Prashun
Sent: Tuesday, November 9, 2004 11:12 PM
To: Alejandro Lopez
Subject: Re: Opinion Needed

So, I'm confused—you recommend Green, then?

From: Lopez, Alejandro
Sent: Tuesday, November 9, 2004 11:13 PM
To: Prashun Thind
Subject: Re: Opinion Needed

Hard to say, now that I think about it.

You do realize, of course, that there's probably a 20% chance that the Jets are this year's version of the Panthers and are going to continue to go house all year long . . . in which case, the Jets-Dolphins game will be a running back's dream, with Martin going for 150 and 2 TDs.

From: Thind, Prashun
Sent: Tuesday, November 9, 2004 11:23 PM
To: Alejandro Lopez
Subject: Re: Opinion Needed

You're killing me. Help a brutha out. Just give me a definitive answer.

From: Lopez, Alejandro
Sent: Tuesday, November 9, 2004 11:40 PM
To: Prashun Thind
Subject: Re: Opinion Needed

Okay. Well, what's the weather supposed to be like? My homey down in Miami said something about a hurricane or "hurricane-like conditions." See anything about that?

From: Thind, Prashun
Sent: Tuesday, November 9, 2004 11:47 PM
To: Alejandro Lopez
Subject: Re: Opinion Needed

Bro, I don't friggin' know.
It's Miami. Hot? Balmy? Caribbean Cool? Blustery?

From: Lopez, Alejandro
Sent: Tuesday, November 9, 2004 11:50 PM
To: Prashun Thind
Subject: Re: Opinion Needed

Fine. I guess if I had to choose, I'd go with Martin. He'll run well against the 'Phins.

From: Thind, Prashun
Sent: Tuesday, November 9, 2004 11:57 PM
To: Alejandro Lopez
Subject: Re: Opinion Needed

Cool. Thanks. I've made up my mind, then.

From: Lopez, Alejandro
Sent: Tuesday, November 9, 2004 11:58 PM
To: Prashun Thind
Subject: Re: Opinion Needed

But I have to say that I like Ahman a lot too. Just because he's had a slow start doesn't mean that you should quit on him. A stud is still a stud, and he and Favre could get hot at the drop of a hat. I'd be lying if I said otherwise.

From: Thind, Prashun
Sent: Tuesday, November 9, 2004 11:59 PM
To: Alejandro Lopez
Subject: Re: Opinion Needed

Al, you're killing me. Stop messing with my mind. I'm set with Martin.

From: Lopez, Alejandro
Sent: Tuesday, November 9, 2004 11:59 PM
To: Prashun Thind
Subject: Re: Opinion Needed

Hey, man. Just trying to help. I feel your pain.
It's a tough call, and I'd hate to guess wrong.

<< WHO DO I START? >>
(W.D.I.S.)

"Life is a sum of all your choices."—Albert Camus

WHO DO I START?

In fantasy football no question is more difficult. Message boards are dedicated to it. Pointless e-mail conversations stem from it. And leagues are won and lost because of it.

Do you start an injured player or a mediocre talent? A veteran or a rookie? Do you go on last minute hunches or do you stick to your guns?

Choose right, and you breathe freely for another week.

Choose wrong, and you'll smack yourself in the forehead.

"Who do I start?" the scared manager asks, which is really the same thing as asking, "What am I doing with my life?" He asks anyone and everyone. But like all existential questions, the answer to W.D.I.S. must be faced alone.

THE "SMELL OF VICTORY" START

One of the main mottos of fantasy football is that you should always Start Your Studs. You should remain loyal. You should believe in proven talent. Even if your boys are underperforming, you stick with them.

IN-SEASON FANTASY FOOTBALL MOTTOS

1. Always start your studs.
2. Never trade with a division rival.
3. Never trade with a team that you still have to face.
4. Always wait until Sunday morning to set your lineup.
5. Never rely on midweek injury reports.
6. Never rely on the four Mikes (Martz, Tice, Holmgren, and Shanahan).
7. Never schedule vacation during fantasy football season.
8. Always start players facing the Browns.
9. Never start players from the Browns.
10. Never, ever trash talk until Monday Night Football is over.

For many years the United States military employed a similar strategy. Lincoln stuck with his boy, Ulysses S. Grant, until the Civil War turned around. Teddy Roosevelt[21] rode his Rough Riders all the way into Mexico. And FDR relied upon General Ike as he stormed into Berlin.

The savvy fantasy football manager typically employs a similar strategy. You line up Priest Holmes, Brett Favre, and Torry Holt, and roll with them. You get behind these guys. Always. And if they have two poor games in a row, so be it. They'll produce eventually.

But sometimes there are exceptions. In the case of the military this strategy worked . . . until Vietnam, when JFK refused to bench Robert S. McNamara. McNamara was Kennedy's golden boy. He was "untradable," a key player. But somewhere, somehow, McNamara lost his winning touch. He carpet bombed, he napalmed, and he was increasingly oblivious to fundamental changes on the ground.

He lost hearts and minds.

---

21. Many have incorrectly attributed the phrase "Speak softly and carry a big stick" to TR. In fact, he was paraphrasing a West African proverb. At any rate, few in the Bush League actually follow his advice.

So too with the fantasy manager who refuses to bench a permanently slumping stud. For whatever reason, the battleground has changed, and his key player will not be returning to form anytime soon.

Take Kordell "Slash" Stewart in 1998. Or Tim Brown in 2002. Or Marshall Faulk in 2004. In their prime, all three players were absolutely devastating. But in those particular years they lost their stud status for good. A manager who can't recognize this fundamental change is in deep trouble.

In the Bush League, Al Lopez is that guy. Earlier in the year he was rolling behind Travis Henry. But now the backfield situation in Buffalo has become murky—yet Lopez refuses to concede that he's lost momentum.

There's an ever-increasing credibility gap. Lopez is stuck in a fantasy football quagmire, and he's too stubborn to admit it.

"Lopez," Thind says, "your boy Henry seems to be losing carries."

"Shut up. He's fine. I'm starting him."

"Al," Schlots says, "you've got Henry splitting carries with McGahee, and Michael Pittman on your bench. Start him instead."

"I'm riding Henry to victory. I repeat: Henry is my starter."

Al Lopez won't accept that the war is already lost. He's like Lieutenant Colonel Bill Kilgore in *Apocalypse Now*—a man fueled by Wagner and a need to find the best waves in Vietnam. Despite the bloodshed and grenades exploding around him, Kilgore remained unfazed.

Lopez won't accept the threat of a new and elusive enemy. He may be able to ride a few more games with Henry, but that won't last forever. McGahee is lurking in the jungle, ready to sniper Lopez and his team. But never mind that for now, because Lopez has taken a big whiff of napalm . . . and it still smells like victory.

THE ALWAYS BET ON BLACK START

Woe is the manager who must choose between players stuck in a running-back-by-committee (aka "RBBC"). Like a nervous gambler working the roulette table in Vegas, this manager is convinced that he can sense patterns.

He might have some early season luck—methodically selecting from a carousel of running backs each week. Wheatley. Crockett. Crockett. Wheatley. He manages to pick the right back each time—he's on a hot streak. But this luck imbues him with a false sense of confidence. He thinks that he can see patterns. Yes, it all makes perfect sense to him.

RECENT DREADFUL RBBCS

1. Amos Zereoue/Chris Fuamatu-Ma'afala/Jerome Bettis
2. Duce Staley/Brian Westbrook/Correll Buckhalter
3. James Jackson/Lee Suggs/William Green
4. Troy Hambrick/Marcel Shipp/Emmitt Smith
5. Travis Minor/Lamar Gordon/Sammy Morris
6. Antowain Smith/Kevin Faulk
7. James Stewart/Artose Pinner

But it only takes a few bad turns of the fantasy wheel—either non-performances by both running backs or the benched player going off while the starting player does nothing—to shake his confidence. Then, predictably, he'll double down on his guy, and he'll be toast.

By midyear The Two-Headed Hydra has managed to corner the market on the Minnesota Vikings backfield, which they claim is "the best ground game in the NFC." But what they haven't realized is that their *starting* running back slot, like the face of a twelve-year-old sans Accutane, won't be clearing up anytime soon.

Initially they're unconcerned. They run down their roster, alternating between the Whizzinator-endorsing Onterrio Smith, the brittle Michael Bennett, and the effective but uninspiring Moe Williams. And just to make sure that their bases are covered, they also secure the talents of the utterly ambiguous Mewelde Moore.

MOST AMUSING DRUG-RELATED ATHLETE RUN-INS WITH THE LAW

1. Onterrio Smith—Tried to pass through airport security with "The Original Whizzinator" and six vials of dried urine. The Whizzinator is a device used to fake drug tests that includes a prosthetic penis attached to a jockstrap and a plastic bag.
2. Qyntel Woods—After being pulled over for speeding, and found with a joint in his car, he handed the police officer his basketball trading card in lieu of his missing driver's license.
3. Todd Marinovich—Former NFL quarterback found by a police officer in a public bathroom with a bent spoon and syringe. Fled on a bicycle, but was arrested fifteen blocks away. On the police report, listed his occupation as "unemployed artist."
4. Tonya Harding—Jacked then-boyfriend in the head with a hub-cap.
5. Nate Newton—Found with 213 pounds of marijuana. Though Nate is a rather large man, this seems excessive.

But the problem is, The Hydra can only start one running back out of this motley crew. They gamble on Onterrio, only to have him split carries with the three other guys, producing terrible fantasy numbers.

No matter. A poor performance only deepens their belief that Smith is now "due." So they add more chips, bet on black, and watch as that little silver ball whirls around.

Never mind that Smith is only getting eight carries per game. Forget that he hasn't had a touchdown in weeks. These things will "average out." Because if they keep doubling down on black, they're bound to win eventually.

Right?

THE MATCHUP-BASED START

Some managers have way too much time on their hands. While others have gone off to the bar or home to their families, these managers sit alone in their offices, sifting through Web sites, hoping to understand something elusive, something impossible—something that even geniuses like Eric Karabell and Scott Engel don't understand.

They're trying to make matchup-based starts. The principle is simple enough: The values of offensive players change based on the defenses they're facing, weather conditions, and other assorted variables. But, as with all forms of information gathering, there's a danger in overanalysis.

Witness Prashun Thind.

He has a strong quarterback in Marc Bulger and a decent but unproven backup in Quincy Carter. For most managers, the choice is easy: Bulger is a consistent top-five performer. Quincy, or "Q" as he's known to his legion of fans, moped around Dallas, scrambled unnecessarily, was cut for snorting coke, and then trundled off to the New York Jets.

In this situation most managers don't think twice—keep Carter on the bench, start Bulger, and watch him go.

But Thind has concerns. Big concerns. Bulger is playing this week at Lambeau Field on Monday night, and a quick study reveals the following: His completion percentage is 5.8 percent worse on grass fields, 8.2 percent worse in outdoor stadiums, 4.2 percent worse during night games, 3.8 percent worse during road games, and a whopping 11.8 percent worse in sub-forty weather conditions.

"Ack," Thind says as he filters this "mad science" into a spreadsheet. So he takes a look at Quincy.

He's playing the Cardinals, on a grass field, in the midafternoon. Most managers would look at this information and shrug. We're talking about Quincy Carter after all, a perennial backup.

But Thind sees a good bit more than that—Q's record against head coach Dennis Green is impressive, the Cardinals' record against East Coast teams that have traveled more than two thousand miles is terrible, and Q's completion is 10 percent higher in games that AccuWeather.com deems "sunny" or "reasonably sunny."

Thind checks the "Tempe Central Bank" webcam.

Like most days in Arizona, it's sunny. Very sunny.

"That's it," Thind declares. "I'm starting Q."

Which leads to a rather puzzled Kwame Jones lobbing in a phone call.

"Thind, you're starting Carter this week? Explain."

"Yep. It's a matchup-based start."

"But you have Bulger—"

"I know my players. I've crunched the numbers. I've done my analysis. And in this particular situation Quincy's just a better fit for the Thindianapolis Colts."

"But he's lousy. He could be matched up against a Pop Warner team and he'd still be lousy."

"Listen, Kwame, when you're big-ballin', come talk to me. Until then I'll keep doing my thang, Thindian-style."

Thind sticks to his guns. Carter starts for his team, and proceeds to throw for a measly 132 yards. Bulger, meanwhile, manages to overcome his matchup problems and goes for 448 and 2 TDs.

But will Thind admit he's wrong? No, never. *"There are simply more variables to crunch,"* he writes to the rest of the Bush League on Tuesday morning. *"No model or spreadsheet is perfect on its own. Thindy Infante will continue to make strategic starts as he sees fit."*

THE OBSCURE START

Some managers love making choices that no one really gets. They're the kind of guys who draft tight ends in the third round—they simply enjoy bucking conventional wisdom.

This manager typically adopted this mindset in high school; he was typically a music junky. He was the guy who stitched a SUICIDAL TENDENCIES patch on his jeans jacket, even though he'd been listening to Wham! a week before. He hated *The Joshua Tree* and despised the Stones because they were simply "too easy to like."

Fifteen years later this guy has joined your league. His team usually isn't in contention, but he has a bevy of semi-interesting players that he's constantly cycling in and out of his lineup.

In the Bush League, O'Brien is this guy. He insists that the rest of the league "lacks vision," "simply doesn't get it," and uses a "lemming-like" approach in making starts. The Mick, on the other hand, prefers to "think outside the box."

ANNOYING BUSINESS BUZZWORDS THAT HAVE INFILTRATED FANTASY FOOTBALL

1. Outside the box
2. The law of diminishing returns
3. The "dead cat" bounce
4. Vaporware
5. Peel the onion
6. Disintermediate
7. Win-win
8. Value-added
9. Tee up
10. Low-hanging fruit

Sure, he could ride Rod Smith as his second wide receiver, but that would be too easy. It's far better to ask the commish if he can use "an ace formation" with tight ends Randy McMichael and Marcus Pollard so that he has "more frequent targets."

Don't try questioning this logic. That will lead nowhere.

"O'Brien," Lopez says, "it seems really counterintuitive to start two tight ends. Don't they score less on average?"

"Yes, in most cases, but this is an exception. . . ."

"An exception? How?"

"I'm seeing what you guys can't see," O'Brien says cryptically, and that is that. The Mick has scoffed at the conventional and made his own obscure starts. Now it's only a matter of time before his "vision" will be fully appreciated.

THE MUTUAL FUND START

The method is as simple as it is boring. Stay calm. Diversify your position. Hedge your bets. Don't assume too much risk. Don't start too many players from the same team. Don't start a defense and a quarterback in the same game. Don't leave yourself exposed. In short: Be Kwame.

THE *WHEN HARRY MET SALLY* START

Certain managers love to go with their old stalwarts, players who've proven reliable in the past. It's like the guy who invites a girl over for a movie, is unsure what she might enjoy, and ends up settling on *When Harry Met Sally*—a safe (albeit uninspired) choice.

MOVIES THAT OUR GIRLFRIENDS AND WIVES MAKE US WATCH

1. *When Harry Met Sally*. Most overrated orgasm in popular cinema.
2. *Terms of Endearment*. "She's in pain. My daughter's in pain. Give her the shot. Do you understand me? Give my daughter the shot!"
3. *Beaches*. "I was jealous of you. I was so jealous I couldn't see straight!"
4. *Love Story*. "Love means never having to say you're sorry."
5. *Pretty Woman*. The most annoying Julia Roberts film of all time. Which is saying something.

. . . AND MOVIES WE'D RATHER BE WATCHING

1. *The Dirty Dozen.* "You've got one religious maniac, one malignant dwarf, two near-idiots, and the rest I don't even wanna think about!"
2. *Full Metal Jacket.* "You had best unf—k yourself or I will unscrew your head and shit down your neck!"
3. *The Usual Suspects.* "The greatest trick the devil ever pulled was convincing the world he didn't exist."
4. *The Good, the Bad and the Ugly.* "When you have to shoot, shoot. Don't talk."
5. *Cool Hand Luke.* "What we got here is a failure to communicate."

Over the last two weeks several running back situations have broken Schlots's way. He's now looking at a backfield surplus that would have Alan Greenspan doing backflips.

But even though Schlots has many exciting options, his natural instinct is to stick with his favorites. He's too nostalgic, and he knows it.

And the Mephistophelean Prashun Thind knows it too. Prash is currently one place behind Schlots in the race to secure a play-off position. And so he figures he'll lob in a call to try to prevent the "Big Guy" from starting an emerging stud.

"What's up, homey?"

"*Nada mucho.* I'm just going over my stable of sweet running backs."

"Figured as much. Which is why I'm calling. I'm just curious to see if you're still sticking with your boy, Emmitt?"

"Gulp," Schlots says. "I don't really know. Right now my backfield is more stacked than Dolly Parton. I'm not sure if ole E-Dawg should really be getting the rock."

For many years Emmitt Smith has been Schlots's favorite player. It's irrational, but Schlots has made an effort to draft or trade for him each of the last four years. There's just something about Emmitt's smile that Schlots views as kind. But the reality is, Emmitt has lost his burst, he's playing for the Cardinals—the French Foreign Legion of fantasy offenses—and Schlots has absolutely no reason to reload his old gun.

"You can't quit on him now," Thind says. "E-Dawg's your boy."

"But I have all these young puppies barking . . ."

"Use them as trade bait."

Schlots is like Homer Simpson staring at a box full of doughnuts. "All right," he concedes. "Fine, I'll do it."

"You'll do what?"

"I'll . . . start . . . Emmitt."

"Well done, laddie," Thind says, his weaselly work of encouraging Schlots to start an inferior running back complete. And poof, just like that, he's gone.

THE WALKING WOUNDED START

Some managers are merely trying to cobble together a viable lineup. Not an impressive lineup, mind you, just a lineup with semihealthy players who can actually limp onto the field.

This isn't always easy. Their rosters have more red crosses than a Somali health clinic. A mediocre player who's "questionable" must be weighed against a talented player who's "doubtful."

Of course, none of these players are destined to do anything of significance. They're like the zombies in Michael Jackson's seminal video, "Thriller," emerging from the sewer, dropping an appendage here or there, and then falling into lockstep behind MJ as he shimmies about.

TOP MICHAEL JACKSON QUOTES

1. "We can fly, you know. We just don't know how to think the right thoughts and levitate ourselves off the ground."
2. "I have been the artist with the longest career, and I am so proud and honored to be chosen from heaven to be invincible."
3. "Why can't you share your bed? The most loving thing to do is to share your bed with someone. It's very charming. It's very sweet. It's what the whole world should do."
4. From the opening lines of the "Thriller" video. Michael: "There's something I've got tell you." Girlfriend: "Yes, Michael." "I'm not like other guys." "Of course you're not. That's why I love you." "No, I mean I'm *different*."

In the Bush League, the manager most likely to face a Walking Wounded Start is Goldman. The reasons for this are simple. First, he drafts older players who are injured by midyear. Then he underbids on free agents. And as the weekly trade deadline approaches, he'll ignore lowball offers and then simply accept that his team will be "rather banged up" come Sunday.

Goldman, of course, will have excuses. But he's embarrassed nonetheless. This weekend, he'll have a blank spot at QB, joined in the backfield by two running backs with swollen knees. He could swap in a "questionable" Mike Alstott, but what would be the point?

Goldman's team is posted up in ER. They're bandaged, battered, and bruised. And far be it from the good doctor to force any of them back onto the field.

THE MASADA START

As strange as this may sound, some managers will start crappy players in order to hurt other managers. Perhaps they're doing this because they're risk-seeking, or perhaps they're sacrificing their team to protect a higher principle.

We're not really sure. All we can tell you is that we check their line-ups on Sunday morning and shake our heads in puzzlement.

Which is exactly what we did when we saw whom The Bitter Drafter was starting at wide receiver. Justin Gage, Arnaz Battle, and Robert Ferguson. They don't exactly inspire fear, but perhaps that's the point. Perhaps he'd rather lose to Lopez with his scrappiest players than win and help O'Brien or Thind in their quest for a league title.

Such behavior is very spiteful, and quite possibly illegal under the Bush League constitution. Some would argue that it's pure collusion. But it's hard to regulate. Who knows whether someone who starts Aaron Shea at tight end is throwing a game? And what are we to make of a guy who slots rookie Eli Manning into his lineup on a "hunch that he'll be Peyton-like"?

We're reminded of Masada, ca. 72 C.E.

After the Romans had conquered most of the holy land, the last surviving Jewish rebels retreated to this mountain refuge. Attempting to finish the resistance, Roman governor Flavius Silva brought in fifteen thousand slaves, built an assault ramp, and moved it toward the defensive walls.

MASADA-START PLAYERS

1. Any rookie quarterback
2. Artose Pinner
3. Tony Hollings
4. Dennis Northcutt
5. Freddie Mitchell

The Jews' fate was sealed. But rather than give in to the Romans, the rebel leader, Eleazer, convinced his people to kill themselves. In the morning the Romans found only dead bodies (except for two women and five children, who'd escaped the mass suicide by hiding in a cave).

This was a grim but proud moment in Jewish history, and it's probably wholly inappropriate to use in the context of fantasy football. And still, we can't help but think of The Bitter Drafter's starts as Masada-esque. He's sacrificing his team on principle, and Thind and O'Brien know it.

"Bitter Drafter, we know that you're sandbagging," implores Thind. *"Please be reasonable."*

"Reasonable? I'm just taking risks."

"There are risks and then there's suicide."

"You manage your team, I'll manage mine."

O'Brien then approaches Kwame and asks for an audit. ("Time for some commissioneering, Kwame.") But Kwame says that these things are "hard to legislate."

Peeved, Thind types an e-mail to the entire league accusing The Bitter Drafter of "lacking class" and "choosing to throw games to upset the otherwise stable balance of the Bush League."

"I'm not throwing games," The Bitter Drafter responds by phone to Thind.

"Oh? Then what are you doing?"

"I'm fighting with honor."

"No, you're fighting with Troy Hambrick in your backfield."

"Listen," The Bitter Drafter says, "I will not cave to your petty demands." Then he hangs up. By the end of the season he'll have no chance of winning any of his games. But damn it all, he's not going to help O'Brien and Thind, and he certainly won't let his players be taken alive.

OTHER W.D.I.S. QUESTIONS

1. **The Twin Dragon Start:** Do you start two receivers from the same team?

2. **The Foul-Weather Start:** Is bad weather better or worse for a running back?

3. **The Champ Bailey Start:** Do you start an average receiver against a great cornerback?

4. **The OK Corral Start:** Will your running back see more or less carries in a shoot-out?

5. **The Cannibalism Start:** Do you start your first-string defense against your first-string quarterback?

6. **The Single-Bar Helmet Start:** Which kicker do you pick? And does it really matter?

7. **The Willis Reed Start:** Do you start a stud with a lingering injury?

8. **The Koren Robinson Start:** Do you start a talented player who may get benched for disciplinary reasons?

9. **The Fear of Success Start:** Do you start a middle-of-the-road player who went off the week before?

10. **The WR3 Dartboard Start:** How do you choose between Ricky Proehl, Doug Gabriel, Corey Bradford, and David Patten?

<< THE MIDSEASON >>
AWARDS CEREMONY

EACH YEAR ON MONDAY NIGHT OF WEEK EIGHT, BUSH
League managers meet for their annual Midseason Awards Ceremony.
For some, this is an opportunity to celebrate early accomplishments.
For others, it's a chance to potshot fellow managers. For all, the
Midseason Awards Ceremony represents a chance to take stock: The
season started a mere two months ago, but it's already half-over.

8:52 P.M.

The Mick strolls into the Bump-N-Run and grabs a large table.
With a giant one-armed sweeping motion, he brushes napkins, plastic
cups, stray french fries, and a crumpled *USA Today* sports section onto
the floor.

A Bumpette gives him the stink eye; he casually stares back.

8:58 P.M.

Kwame, Schlots, and Thind enter the bar. "Fellas," Kwame says, "I
trust everyone is ready for the Midseason Awards Ceremony. As you
know, all Bush League members voted on each award after the first

seven games of the season, the votes were tabulated, and we have our winners—or losers, as the case may be."

9:00 P.M.

The broadcast for the New York Jets–Miami Dolphins game begins. The Bush League table loudly sings the "Dah, dah, dah, dah" Monday Night Football theme song.

9:02 P.M.

"The Thindianapolis Colts will be the big winner tonight," Thind says. "I'm like the fantasy football equivalent of Ron Howard."

The Mick throws several crushed peanut shells at Thind.

Schlots takes Thind's beer and pounds it. He then returns the empty glass with his frothy backwash to Thind, places Thind's hand around it, and tips his dirty white hat.

9:09 P.M.

ABC shows the first close-up of an already beleaguered Coach Dave Wannstedt. "Schlots," says Kwame, "I never realized this before, but you've got a Wannstedt mustache. That's a porn mustache!"

"That's precisely what I'm going for, Kwame," responds Schlots. He then strokes the mustache slowly between his thumb and forefinger.

9:17 P.M.

Goldman sidles up to the table and exhales loudly. He's still in his hospital-issued pink pastel scrubs.

"Well, that's a lovely shade of bitch," observes The Mick.

The Two-Headed Hydra comes in a few minutes later, but no one recognizes them. "Who are you?" Kwame asks.

"We're Two-Headed Hydra. We're in your league."

"You are?"

"Yep! You e-mail us every day."

"But how did you get in the league?"

"We knew Dave Pazamona."

"Yeah, Dave's not in the league anymore."

"Yep! We know."

Kwame, embarrassed, buys them both beers.

GOOFIEST NFL COACHES

1. Rich Kotite
2. Dave Wannstedt
3. Steve Spurrier
4. Dave Campo
5. Wayne Fontes
6. Wade Phillips
7. Dick Jauron
8. Vince Tobin
9. Dave McGinnis
10. Mike Tice

9:18 P.M.

During a commercial Kwame stands up. "All right, gentlemen, here we go . . ."

The Wheels Coming Off the Wagon Award: Goes to the team hurtling toward collapse and elimination from Bush League contention. An iffy draft, a slew of injuries, and an inability to play the free-agent market have contributed to this team's demise. In recent weeks this team has sunk even lower than The Bitter Drafter's squad. It's swerving across the fantasy football highway, losing control. That team is . . . Team Goyim.

"I can't argue with this award," concedes Adam. "I've flailed my way to a 2–5 record so far, and I don't see it getting any better. Between the hospital and the wedding, I lack the tools to repair Team Goyim's banged-up chassis."

9:32 P.M.

Stuart Scott is prowling the stands, asking insipid questions of a player's mother. She wears the player's jersey, a significant amount of jewelry, and has a pom-pom on her head. Scott barely listens to her response, and instead offers "Big Ups!" to some unknown rapper. Al Michaels sighs. The Bump-N-Run collectively groans.

9:35 P.M.

Another commercial break. "It's with a certain degree of disappointment that I present the following award."

> **The Lightning in a Bottle Award:** Goes to the team that made the best draft pick the latest in the draft. This year the long written-off Curtis Martin was taken in the fifth round. The Jets running back, a player no one wanted, is currently leading the NFL in rushing. The winner of this award, therefore, is . . . the Thindianapolis Colts.

"The only person not surprised by the phoenixlike rise of CuMar is yours truly," crows Prashun Thind. "This is textbook Thindianapolis Colts team-building and, I trust, a blueprint that many in the Bush League will follow in future years. Never give up hope, never quit on—"

"Please, someone, shut him up," O'Brien says.

Kwame makes a calming motion with his hands.

Reluctantly Thind sits down. But he doesn't stop grinning at O'Brien.

MOST-IRRITATING OCCURRENCES AT SPORTING EVENTS

1. The Wave
2. The Applause Meter
3. Interviews with players' wives
4. People on cell phones mugging for TV cameras
5. The miniblimp that drops candy into the crowd, creating riots over said candy
6. Semi-buff gymnastic guys slingshotting T-shirts into stands
7. Old people wearing headbands
8. The pyrotechnics that accompany Europe's "The Final Countdown" during a play-off game
9. Dueling section chants: "Go!" . . . "Steelers!"
10. The Tomahawk Chop or any other mocking-of-Native-Americans arm motion
11. Referee getting into fake fight with mascot
12. Animated scoreboard races involving dots, hot dogs, or trains
13. Courtside fans who high-five players
14. Guys who propose to their girlfriends over the Jumbo-tron
15. Thunder-sticks

10:04 P.M.

Thind is struck in the forehead by more peanut shells.

Marty Booker catches a 3-yard dump pass for a first down. It's a routine play. He promptly drops to one knee and does the annoying thrust-forward-with-one-arm move to signify a first down. "Frickin' hate that guy," says Kwame.

OVERUSED GESTURES BY PROFESSIONAL ATHLETES

1. Throat-cutting gesture
2. Darius Miles and Quentin Richardson's double-head bonk after routine plays
3. Postgame taking-a-knee for the Lord
4. Quarterbacks "silencing the crowd" in a relatively quiet stadium
5. Safeties and cornerbacks making the "incomplete" sign after a wide receiver flubs an easy catch
6. Jersey pulled to reveal heart
7. Jersey snapping à la *Pimp My Ride*
8. Daunte Culpepper's rumba arm motion
9. Any Lambeau Leap done in a stadium that's not Lambeau Field
10. Any end zone celebration that involves a prop
11. Dismissive head-shaking after a running back has broken through two tackles
12. The Donovan McNabb moonwalk
13. Anything that Terrell Owens does
14. "Raising the roof"
15. Defensive lineman dancing a jig

10:27 P.M.

Kwame looks down at his clipboard. "Ah, yes, I enjoy this one."

The Dot-Bomb Award: Goes to the team that made the worst draft pick. That player is the nearly invisible Lee Suggs. He was inexplicably taken in the third round based on an unaccountable series of mock drafts and loads of preseason hype. The man who drafted him: The Mick.

"Screw all of you, and in particular, screw that old guy sitting at the bar who's been looking at me funny all night. Lee Suggs wasn't any worse than a bunch of your picks, was he?" The Mick is met by silence. "Goldman, you flailed in the third round too." Goldman shrugs. "And besides, the season isn't over. The Mick feels good about Suggs breaking out. The Mick likes Suggs."

"Whatever you say, Sam Bowie," chirps Thind.

10:30 P.M.

Kwame clinks his glass with a fork. "This award is sure to draw some groans, but the Bush League has always given credit where credit is due."

The Stealing Candy from a Baby Award: Goes to the team that pulled the biggest fleece trade. That trade was the much maligned but ultimately commissioner-approved swap of Torry Holt for Chris Brown, David Patten, and Antwaan Randle El. The perennial loser in this trade was the guppy team extraordinaire, The Two-Headed Hydra. The winner in this trade—as if there was ever any question—was the Latin land-shark, El Matador.

"Because Al Lopez is not here to accept his award in person, I will read a prepared statement from him," says Kwame. "It reads: On behalf of my wife and child, we thank you for your kind support. We credit the trade for our electric 6–1 start to the season. I look forward to further productive trade talks down the stretch."

"Okay," Kwame says, "moving on . . ."

"Wait," Thind says.

"What."

"We haven't heard from Hydra."

"Oh, right. Sorry. Does The Hydra wish to speak?"

"That's okay," says one.

"We're good," says the other.

10:55 P.M.

"It's getting late, Monday Night Football is boring, so let's get on with it . . ."

The Stanley Kowalski Award: Named after the lead from *A Streetcar Named Desire,* who said, "to hold front position in this rat race, you've got to believe you're lucky." Gentlemen, we *know* this guy is lucky. How else could he be 5–2 despite having scored the fewest points in the league? Of course, you know that I'm speaking of . . . John Schlots.

Schlots stands up. "Thank you, thank you. But, of course, my good friend Kwame is only half-right. Luck is 50 percent inspiration and 30 percent, uh, motivation, and . . . it's good to be king."

He grins, tips his cap, and sits down.

11:02 P.M.

"Okay, next up we have the only award where the voting was unanimous."

The Wilt Chamberlain Award: Named after the manager who screwed the most managers in the shortest amount of time. This manager jacked people by taking backups, he's refused to trade, and he went out of his way to basically ruin everyone's season. Y'all know who this is . . . The Bitter Drafter.

"Because The Bitter Drafter is not here in person to accept his award, I'll read an e-mail from him," says Kwame. "It reads: I don't care about the Bush League. And I certainly don't care about the Bush League Midseason Awards Ceremony. Go to hell."

11:05 P.M.

"Ah yes, and the final award of the evening is a sympathy award. And, in this case, a personal one."

The Snakebit Award: Goes to the team that has suffered through the most close, unlucky losses. The team is, in a word, snakebit—a good team that manages to lose more than it should. Despite repeated suggestions by The Mick that he's the unluckiest guy in the league, the winner of this award goes to . . . Kwame Jones, Inc.

"I appreciate everyone's sympathy, and know that it is truly heartfelt," says Kwame. "But don't cry for me, Argentina. I remain strong, and will fight through these tough four losses. Kwame Jones, Inc., won't panic. We'll continue to fight."

11:44 P.M.

Jay Fiedler, playing for nothing in a Jets blowout, drops back and tosses his second straight interception. The lone remaining Miami fan in the bar rips off his aquamarine Dolphins jersey.

"Hey, pal," The Mick says, "tell Fiedler that Shabbat is over."

No answer.

"It's no longer the day of rest."

"My dick, your ass," the Dolphins fan responds.

The Bush League table grows quiet. The Mick smiles uneasily.

11:45 P.M.

"Well, that's my cue. I'm out," says Goldman.

"Dude, there's still seven minutes left in the game," says Thind.

"No, Goldman's right," Kwame says. "This game is beat."

"Yup, The Mick is out."

The men shove their chairs back, stand in unison, and exit the Bump-N-Run.

17

<< ZEN AND THE ART >> OF TALKING TRASH

SOME MANAGERS PLAY FANTASY FOOTBALL FOR THE COM- petition, some use the season to strengthen friendships, and some simply want to talk a little smack.

Ah, trash talk: the lifeblood of fantasy football.

Is there anything sweeter than spending an hour crafting the ultimate taunting e-mail? Is there anything finer than mocking Trent Dilfer's owner as he lobs a wounded duck? And is there anything more satisfying than writing a paean in "support" of a manager on a three-game losing streak?

In the Bush League, trash-talking isn't just a vital form of communication—it's the ultimate form of self-expression. An art form, if you will. A masterpiece painted on a canvas of smack.

RICKY HENDERSON AND THE ART OF THE THIRD PERSON

Great trash talkers often speak in the third person. There's no grammatical or Old English precedent behind this. Rather, it's used largely to infuriate those around them.

Among the pantheon of inspired self-promotional third-person trash talkers, Ricky Henderson reigns supreme. Ricky *always* referred to himself as Ricky. And while some of his peers, like Bo Jackson, spoke in the third person with a wink, a nod, and a clever marketing campaign, Ricky seemed unaware that this manner of speaking was both irksome and arrogant.

So when Ricky broke Lou Brock's record for most stolen bases, he immodestly proclaimed that he was "the greatest of all time." Insightful analysis from Ricky—and this coming from the same guy who once framed a signed million-dollar signing-bonus check and hung it on his wall.

While everyone in the Bush League revels in Ricky-esque third-person smack, no one utilizes this style as much as Chris O'Brien. There is no "we" in Chris O'Brien's speech, or even an "I." There's only the The Mick doing this or The Mick doing that.

Try asking him what he did on Friday.

"The Mick made the greatest free-agent pickup. Ever."

How about Saturday?

"The Mick was being The Mick. He was preparing in Mick-like fashion."

How about Sunday?

"The Mick will be watching his team dom-i-nate."

Listening to him rattle on like this is comparable to hearing nails scratching a chalkboard. Please, Lord, make it stop.

WOODY ALLEN AND THE ART OF SELF-DEPRECATION

If Woody Allen played fantasy football (and we have little reason to suspect that he does), he'd win many allies with his trademark line: "My one regret in life is that I am not someone else." He makes an interesting point, and one that more than a few of us have considered.

WOODY-ISMS

1. "I can't listen to that much Wagner. I start getting the urge to conquer Poland."
2. "If it turns out that there is a God, I don't think that he's evil. But the worst that you can say about him is that basically he's an underachiever."
3. "Organized crime in America takes in over forty billion dollars a year and spends very little on office supplies."
4. "How is it possible to find meaning in a finite world, given my waist and shirt size?"
5. "As the poet said, 'Only God can make a tree'—probably because it's so hard to figure out how to get the bark on."

Self-deprecation can be an important tool for a fantasy football manager. It deflates your critics' most severe attacks, and allows you to subtly cheap-shot others with an "aw shucks" cloak.

Though not a Jew, and, discouragingly, an avid eater of blueberry bagels, Schlots likes to use Woody Allen's sense of self-mockery to his advantage. Last week, after notching a win against the "vastly superior" Cuban Missile Crisis, he fired off this e-mail:

> In a Hollywood ceremony last night, John Schlotterbeck graciously accepted the Stanley Kowalski Award. In an event designed to reward the least talented yet luckiest people of the year, Schlots was the toast of the party.
>
> The ceremony was not without controversy, however. Paris, distraught over a fat/ugly/midwestern oaf winning her award, screamed at the producers. "It is, like, such a disappointment to give this award to John after honoring previous winners: John Stamos and Posh Beckham." The selection

> committee disagreed, stating "Paris's disappointment only
> confirmed that we picked the right guy."

Lopez reads the e-mail. He shakes his head and reads it again. He then prints it out and reads it a third time, to see if he's missing some sort of joke or insight.

He is not.

Schlots's e-mail is neither funny nor well written. It's just a poor attempt at humor. The message is evil in its simplicity: I'm a humble, modestly talented salt-of-the-earth guy who doesn't take himself too seriously.

And you lost to me.

JOE NAMATH AND THE ART OF CALLING YOUR SHOT

Every so often, underdogs get inspired. They lose their timidity and decide to launch a verbal salvo. "Hell," they figure, "we've been listening to this garbage for weeks—we're due."

Such was the way of Joe Namath, who had the audacity to predict a win against the heavily favored Baltimore Colts in Super Bowl III. This was the Broadway Joe we loved, and not the Broadway Joe who later (drunkenly) said to Suzy Kolber, "I want to kiss you" on national television. (That was a different kind of "upset.")

Last week The Two-Headed Hydra knocked off Goldman, and now they're confident that they can run their winning streak to *two* games.

This Sunday they're facing the vastly superior Kwame Jones, Inc. But no matter, The Hydra feels things clicking into place. So they craft their own brand of bizarre passive-aggressive trash talk: *"Our season has been a disaster, and we suck right now. But there is good news. We picked up our first win, and we're ready to turn things around. We're now gearing up for an inspirational turnaround the likes of which this league has never seen. The Hydra is doing something we do in only the most desperate and rare cases: We're calling our shot. Against all odds we will beat Kwame Jones, Inc."*

The proclamation is met with the sound of crickets. No one cares. No one takes The Two-Headed Hydra seriously. But they have called their shot nonetheless. And they're fired up.

MUHAMMAD ALI AND THE ART OF RIDICULE

No one was—or will ever be—a better trash talker than Muhammad Ali. He is the Alpha and Omega of smack.

Though we could spend months reviewing our favorite Ali lines, we focus on the moment when he used trash-talking repeatedly to embarrass an opponent, Ernie Terrell. He was a sad sack who, despite repeated warnings, insisted on calling Ali by his non-Muslim name, Cassius Clay.

ALI-ISMS

1. "Frazier is so ugly that he should donate his face to the U.S. Bureau of Wildlife."
2. "I am the astronaut of boxing. Joe Louis and Dempsey were just jet pilots. I'm in a world of my own."
3. "I'll beat him so bad he'll need a shoehorn to put his hat on."
4. "I'm so fast that last night I turned off the light switch in my hotel room and was in bed before the room was dark."
5. "When you are as great as I am it is hard to be humble."

Ali was irate. He took his Muslim name seriously. So rather than knocking Terrell out quickly, he kept flicking cutting jabs and yelling, "What's my name, fool? What's my name?"

In the Bush League, The Bitter Drafter refused to call The Death

Maiden by her preferred title, choosing instead to refer to her as "that girl." Big mistake. As they squared off in week eight, for the first time ever, The Death Maiden appeared on Bush League e-mail chains:

"It's 1:45 and The Death Maiden leads 43–14. Please apologize."

"Whatever, girl."

"It's 3:35 and The Death Maiden leads 75–20. Call me by my name."

"No. Girl."

"The Death Maiden wins. Call me Death Maiden. Now."

"No. Never."

This exchange went on for over a day, with The Death Maiden landing a series of withering blows. The Bitter Drafter finally succumbed under the barrage.

STEVEN WRIGHT AND THE ART OF THE SUBTLE CRACK

Adam Goldman hates crude smack talk, opting instead for more subtle taunts. Whether anyone else in the league understands his wisecracking is another matter.

Goldman's style reminds us of the work of Steven Wright—he of the legendary wisecracks that make little sense: "I bought some batteries, but they weren't included. So I had to buy them again."

Like Wright, Goldman prefers to make people chuckle first without fully understanding the humor behind his smack. Last week he suffered an irritating loss to The Hydra. No one loses to The Hydra. And when they do, others are sure to potshot the loser for his ineptitude. In this case, The Mick hurled some brutish albeit uninspired smack, and Goldman was forced to respond.

"O'Brien, precision is the soul of wit."

"So?"

"You're exhibiting Ned Flanders–like soul."

"Dude, you lost to The Hydra. Suck it up."

"Oh, I'm sucking, O'Brien. I'm a Hoover, baby. And you're the Hoover Dam—let the water flow."

The rest of the Bush League read Goldman's comments, chuckled largely out of the assumption that it was funny, then paused to figure out what, exactly, he was saying.

Prashun, who follows all of Goldman's thoughts and movements diligently, was the first to call and respond.

"Goldman, what on earth did any of that mean?"

"If you don't know, you better ask somebody."

"I did ask somebody. They couldn't explain it."

"It's Zen smack. You better meditate on it, and perhaps then its meaning will become clear."

"I'm sorry. I just don't follow your smack logic."

"Maybe you don't. And . . . maybe you don't."

There's silence on the phone. Prashun is not making any progress on decoding Goldman's trash talk. Goldman is not inclined to explain it to him. And it's entirely possible that none of it means anything.

LED ZEPPELIN, A TUB OF BEANS, AND THE ART OF EXCESS

If you've been in a league for more than five years, you've likely heard every taunt, swear word, and ill-conceived analogy known to man. Poor taste is yesterday's news. Jokes have been buried, disinterred, and buried again.

It's easy to become jaded.

The same thing happens with rock bands. You can't commit the same debaucheries night after night. That would be ordinary. That would be boring. And rock stars simply cannot be boring.

The members of Mötley Crüe mainlined Jack Daniel's. Ozzy Osbourne, while wearing a dress, urinated in public. And Led Zeppelin's Jimmy Page allegedly canoodled with groupies in a tub full of refried beans, and later had an "incident" with a red snapper in Seattle.

At some point, though, even the most creative star runs out of ideas.

In fantasy football, as in the world of rock, it's very, very hard to keep coming up with fresh material. But that doesn't stop Prashun Thind from trying. Each season he cycles through offensive trash-talking material before he finally pushes the boundaries of good taste.

"I have given my team specific instructions this weekend," Thind writes Goldman. *"First my stud running back will spike the ball in the end zone. And then he'll dance around a little. I don't know—maybe he'll dunk the ball over the goalpost. Maybe he'll take a knee and pray. But that's just when the fun begins. While your team is waiting around . . . he'll take a razor blade and cut off the skin of your defensive backs. Then he'll wear your defensive back's skin, do a moonwalk in the end zone, and shout, 'I am a loser!' Then he'll take your DB's skin off, he'll take a shower, and he'll use your dried DB skin as a towel . . ."*

And so it goes.

For five pages.

Ending inexplicably with the phrase "Hooker's Cervix."

Goldman stops reading, as does the rest of the Bush League. There's nothing new here except the bare face of depravity. Prash has taken the road to excess. Eventually the fun must end.

<< THE WAR CHEST >>

THE FOLLOWING PHONE CONVERSATION OCCURRED
between Commissioner Kwame Jones and one manager of The Two-
Headed Hydra (though we cannot say which) regarding the Bush
League's weekly free-agent market.

> **Kwame Jones:** Mr. Hydra. Or is it The Hydra? Or just
> Hydra? I'm not sure what we're calling you these days.
> **Hydra:** "Hydra" is good.
> **Kwame:** Right. Hydra, I'm calling to check in about your
> current starting lineup.
> **Hydra:** What's wrong with it?
> **Kwame:** Many things. But first and foremost, it's incomplete.
> **Hydra:** It is?
> **Kwame:** Yeah. You're missing a tight end.
> **Hydra:** Oh, that's right. We ran into a bit of a problem with
> our tight ends. It turns out that they share the same bye
> week. So we can't start either of them.
> **Kwame:** I noticed that, Hydra. That's the trick with bye
> weeks. You can't start a player if he's out on a bye week.
> That's why he has a bye.

Hydra: Good point.

Kwame: Maybe you should consider bidding on a free-agent tight end, *any* free-agent tight end, and drop him into your starting lineup for the week. To remain competitive and all.

Hydra: Can you hold on a second?

Kwame: Sure.

Kwame: Hydra?

Kwame: Hydra?

Hydra: Sorry. Back. So we talked it over.

Kwame: And?

Hydra: And we don't think it's a good use of our free-agent dollars.

Kwame: But you haven't picked up a single free agent yet this season.

Hydra: We're waiting for the right guy to come along. The perfect fit.

Kwame: So you're stockpiling free-agent dollars?

Hydra: Exactly. Building a war chest, if you will.

Kwame: All right, listen—as Commissioner I don't really care about your free-agent war chest strategy. But I *do* have to make sure that every team fields a complete starting lineup. It's not fair to the rest of the league if teams aren't playing at full strength.

Hydra: Fair point, Commish. But our hands are tied.

Kwame: How so?

Hydra: We're war-chesting—not sure what we can do.

Kwame: Simple. Pick up a rent-a-tight-end. Bid the minimum for some guy that no one else wants. Your war chest will remain virtually unscathed.

Hydra [Pauses]: Hold on. Let us think about it.

Kwame: Cool.

Hydra: Okay. Back.

Kwame: And?

Hydra: Sorry, no can do. Our war chest is too important. We can't destabilize our war chest.

Kwame: You must.

Hydra: We can't.

Kwame: Hydra, name a tight end, and I'll give him to you guys for the minimum free-agent bid. Just pick a tight end.

Hydra: Fine. We'll take Lorenzo Neal.

Kwame: Who?

Hydra: Lorenzo Neal. Think he plays for the Chargers.

Kwame: Lorenzo Neal is a fullback. Not a tight end.

Hydra: He blocks, doesn't he? How is that any different from selecting a tight end? Just give us Lorenzo.

Kwame: I can't. He's not considered a tight end. Pick any other tight end. How about Itula Mili, tight end for the Seahawks?

Hydra: Weird name. You sure he's in the NFL?

Kwame: Yeah, he's in the NFL. I'm giving him to you. Okay?

Hydra: Fine. Though we'd really prefer to not start anybody.

Kwame: That's not an option.

Hydra: Then we'll take your guy. Give us Itula Mili. We want Mili.

<< FREE AGENCY >>

EVERYONE LOVES A GARAGE SALE. YOU NEVER KNOW what you'll find. Maybe you'll score some decent bric-a-brac, or perhaps your childhood Leif Garrett record. And if you look closely enough, you may even find something of real value: estate jewelry, an antique watch, or a scuffed pair of snakeskin boots.

ALL VH1'S "WHERE ARE THEY NOW?" FIRST TEAM

1. Leif Garrett
2. Vanilla Ice
3. Ross Perot
4. Bernard Goetz
5. Nick Lachey

The hunt for fantasy football free agents is similar. Managers spend hours sifting through potential acquisitions, hunting for diamonds in the rough, jockeying with other bargain shoppers to land invaluable, season-changing additions.

But buyer beware: You could just as easily end up with junk—an odd planter, a broken dehumidifier, or a VCR that gobbles up the tape of your eleventh-grade prom party.

ALL-TIME BUSH LEAGUE FREE-AGENT PICKUPS

1. **Kurt Warner, 1999**—Went from NFL Europe to starting Rams QB, and posted over 4,300 yards and 41 touchdowns in one of the more dominating fantasy QB seasons ever.
2. **Stephen Davis, 1999**—A backup running back who, until that season, was best known for getting decked by wide receiver Michael Westbrook after Davis directed a homophobic slur at Westbrook. Postbeating, Davis emerged to grind out 1,500 combined yards and 17 touchdowns.
3. **Olandis Gary/Mike Anderson/Clinton Portis/Reuben Droughns**—Doesn't matter who gets slotted in, a Bronco running back will run wild.
4. **Anquan Boldin, 2003**—A relatively unheralded rookie wide receiver on the perennial fantasy graveyard Arizona Cardinals put up over 1,300 yards and 8 touchdowns.
5. **Antonio Gates, 2004**—Came out of nowhere playing for the usually moribund San Diego offense, caught nearly 1,000 yards and a league record 13 tight end touchdowns.

THE MARK CUBAN PICKUP

No real sports-team owner is more like a fantasy football manager than Mark Cuban. He can't dress, sports a horrendous haircut (shouldn't a billionaire have a stylist?), and constantly tinkers with his team.

"The sport of business is the ultimate competition. It's 7x24x365xforever," writes Cuban on blogmaverick.com. We're not entirely sure what this formula equates to, nor are we clear why a billionaire feels the need to blog. But his statement speaks to his unrelenting commitment to building and improving his team.

And he does it all with money, money, and more money. Team chemistry isn't an issue. Never mind that the Mavs have too many guys who can't play defense—Cuban keeps buying. He won't stop until his team is stacked top to bottom with good-on-paper all-stars.

In real life, this leads to a team that jacks up tons of threes before exiting in the first round of the play-offs, but in the world of fantasy football, such a strategy can lead to pure gold. It's a simple formula: Cast a wide net, search actively for emerging starters, and use every spare free-agent dollar to find season-changing players.

MOST COMMON USES OF FREE-AGENT DOLLARS

1. Add ten dollars to a trade to satisfy a guppy.
2. Overspend early on a (new) RBBC.
3. Drop an utterly uninspiring fifteen to twenty dollars on a tight end.
4. Spend serious cash (forty to eighty dollars) on emerging starters.
5. Leave cash in the bank, only to discover at season's end that free-agent dollars have as much real-world value as Monopoly money.

Managers who employ the Mark Cuban Pickup look for emerging starters in great offenses. Take the Saint Louis Rams in 1999. Trent Green was the quarterback of the future but was suddenly lost for the season with a knee injury. Coach Dick Vermeil wept, and wept for a reason. He feared that his offense was doomed. But in stepped Kurt Warner, an alumnus of the now defunct Iowa Barnstormers of the Arena Football League.

Fantasy football managers had one week to make that pickup. Or less. Those who did probably had a starting quarterback already but elected to stock the fridge. And stock the fridge they did: Warner would go on to post historic numbers that year, and owners who made the Mark Cuban Pickup most likely won their leagues.

Those who didn't missed out.

Al Lopez rarely misses out. He's a denizen of the free-agent market, a man who makes and remakes his team in weeks seven, eight, and nine with Mark Cuban Pickups.

When asked by Thind and O'Brien about his free-agent Midas touch, Lopez responds, "Finding that hot free agent before anyone else has spotted him is a lot like my days of ball-hawking freshman ladies at USC."

"Pray tell," says Thind.

"Well, I had a friend who produced the annual freshman face book. He'd give me an advance copy, and I'd 'analyze' it for up-and-comers. So, I'd work from the face book, find smoking-hot freshman girls, swoop down, and do the Humpty Dance.[22] That was my move back then. The ladies didn't know what hit 'em."

"And then what?" asks Thind.

"And then I'd take them out of circulation."

"They weren't stamps, Lopez."

"Semantics, Prash. The bottom line is that it's all about talent recognition, opportunity assessment, and execution."

"That strikes me as buzzardlike," says Thind. "Did you make a *cawww*ing sound while perched above the freshman dorms?"

---

22. Digital Underground's "The Humpty Dance" has one of the better lines in hip-hop: "I like my beats funky, I'm spunky. I like my oatmeal lumpy." And it also features a then little-known backup dancer named Tupac Shakur.

"Dude, try pink flamingo. I was a freaking pink flamingo. Regal looking, bro. I was poised on one leg, staring around, quietly pecking at various food sources. And looking pretty. That's what I do."

"Yeah," says Thind. "I wouldn't know anything about that."

"No, Prash, I don't imagine you would. Ball-hawking doesn't seem to be your game. You seem to be more of a low-hanging-fruit guy."

"One man's catfish is another man's curry, El Matador."

Culinary diversity aside, Lopez's mastery of free agency is no fluke. He does his homework. But more important, when it comes to free agents, he's willing to be aggressive. He takes them out of circulation.

Mark Cuban would be proud.

THE INSPECTOR CLOUSEAU PICKUP

The genius of Inspector Clouseau is that he never gave an inch amid his relentless bumbling. He never once conceded that he was a fool. When criticized for missing an obvious clue, he responded, "I know zat, you i-di-ote." And in the end, things always broke his way. The case was solved, and his reputation and ego were preserved.

Schlots is the Inspector Clouseau of the Bush League's free-agent market. He falls bass-ackwards into his pickups. Sure he occasionally targets a player at a particular position to plug a specific hole. But in most instances Schlots is just as likely to let fly with a near random pickup that serves no purpose whatsoever.

This week, despite having a plethora of grinders, Schlots has locked onto the Broncos' fourth-string running back, Reuben Droughns.

Kwame finds this move peculiar. For sheer amusement he lobs in a call to investigate. "Schlots, I see you grabbed Reuben Droughns."

"Word up, Kwame. I'm excited to have him on board."

"Weird. You have a loaded backfield, and you have your usual assortment of semi-promising rookies. Why add a seventh running back? He's only going to occupy space on your roster. What's the thinking there?"

"No real thinking. Call it a hunch."

"I see."

"I just like Droughns. First, the Reuben is my favorite sandwich; that counts for something. Second, I like his spirit; he's an underdog. Kind of like me. Droughns belongs on The Fat Minnesota Guys."

"Fair enough. But it seems pretty random to me."

"Nothing's random in this life, Kwame. Reuben is on my team for a reason."

And here's the kicker of it all: Schlots gets completely lucky with Droughns, who somehow manages to work his way up the Denver depth chart. A few Quentin Griffin fumbles here, a Mike Anderson pulled groin there, and a sprinkling of Shanahan voodoo dust results in Droughns becoming one of the Bush League's hottest running backs.

Schlots pats himself on the back for his "visionary" personnel move. The rest of the league harrumphs about his "luck" and "idiocy."

His indifference to his surroundings is amazing, his arrogance spectacular, and that's what makes his free-agent pickups so Closeau-like:

> **Housekeeper:** "You've ruined that piano!"
> **Clouseau:** "What is the price of one piano, compared to the terrible crime that has been committed here?"
> **Houekeeper:** "But that's a priceless Steinway."
> **Clouseau [Pauses]:** "Not anymore."

Self-assurance in the face of sheer ineptitude. Once again, the Clouseau Pickup has been made.

THE HINDENBURG PICKUP

On May 6, 1937, the *Hindenburg* blimp, the largest airship ever built, floated above the Lakehurst Naval Air Station in New Jersey. It was the pride of the Third Reich—a gleaming silver orb that was a marvel of aeronautics.

Hundreds gathered to watch as it prepared to land. But then disaster struck: A flame appeared on the outer fin, and within thirty-four seconds, the entire airship was consumed by fire.

As it turns out, the "infallible" German engineers had designed a flying time-bomb, waiting to explode. And while the machinations of free agency lack the gravity of one of the great disasters of the twentieth century, there are some parallels.

For every hyped free agent who goes on to post incredible numbers, there are ten others who look great and are hotly pursued but who quickly explode in a cloud of fiery debris.

ALL-TIME BUSH LEAGUE FREE-AGENT BUSTS

1. Lamar Gordon, Miami Dolphins
2. Ben Gay, Dallas Cowboys
3. Rick Mirer, Oakland Raiders
4. Freddie Mitchell, Philadelphia Eagles
5. Daniel Graham, New England Patriots

Prashun Thind is a frequent victim of the Hindenburg Pickup. He can't help himself. He loves bright, glittery new things. And Prash is so confident, so proud, so infinitely self-assured about his scouting prowess, he'll aggressively pursue his guys to the ends of the earth.

"Gentlemen," Thind announces to the Bush League, *"the Thindianapolis Colts have found our free-agent prodigy. We've arranged our chips in five symmetrical color-coded stacks, and we . . . are . . . all-in."*

"Thind," The Mick e-mails back, *"if your track record is any indication, you're about to overpay for your usual sack of potatoes. I scoff in your general direction."*

And who, pray tell, is Thind's free-agent prodigy? Why, it's none other than Derrick Blaylock—a little-known second-stringer on the

Kansas City Chiefs. A backup who theoretically may start in place of the gimpy Priest Holmes.

Thind proceeds to bid a whopping one hundred forty dollars for his guy. This is a bullish move. Thind is pumping hydrogen into his blimp, watching in awe as it floats up.

His thinking is not without merit. Holmes, the most dominant running back in fantasy football, has a bad hip that could sideline him for a considerable period of time. If Thind can swoop in and grab the new starter, it could be a lucrative pickup.

"Could be big for you, Thind, could be big," says Lopez. Unlike the ever-ornery O'Brien, Lopez respects Thind's free-agency kung fu.

"All visionaries start with a dream to change the world."

"You're not changing the world, you're making a pickup."

"Well, with this pickup I'm at least changing the Bush League."

Alas, Prash's confidence is unfounded. Blaylock proves to be a one-week wonder. He runs wild for a game or two before getting dinged up himself. And in steps *his* replacement, Larry Johnson, who posts staggering numbers for the rest of the season.

Blaylock was a high-priced dud.

The idea was right—and still, Thind's project exploded before his very eyes. And with that the bulk of Prash's free-agent dollars goes up in smoke. The briefly sparkling image of Derrick Blaylock—the next great thing—is now a burning husk, flames twisting in the wind as he plummets down to earth.

THE PETS.COM PICKUP

Some managers simply don't understand market fundamentals. They don't check message boards to see who's hot and who's not. And they don't place calls or write e-mails to gage interest in a potential pickup. So when the rest of the league bids within five dollars of a desired target, they miss by forty.

In the Bush League The Two-Headed Hydra doesn't understand the relative value of free agents. They're like investors who bought shares of Pets.com based on three scoops of Purina Dog Chow and loads of hype. Everyone else could sniff out a sham, but not them. They were carried away, buying what was interesting to them—valuation be damned.

"Gentlemen," Kwame announces this week, *"Hydra has successfully attained the services of free-agent wide receiver Jabar Gaffney. Their winning bid was ninety-five free-agent dollars. The next, closest bid was—wait for it, wait for it—zero free-agent dollars."*

The Hydra's confused. Gaffney should be a hot commodity. They'd built their war chest to secure the services of players like Gaffney. They even discussed this with Commissioner Kwame. Why didn't anyone else bid high for him? Why hadn't anyone else bid on him at all?

"Hydra," Lopez says, *"Gaffney should have paid you to be on your team."*

Thind adds, *"Who on earth is Jabar Gaffney?"*

"We're happy to get our guy. Whatever the cost," responds The Hydra.

Sadly, no one doubts that.

THE DEAD-ENDER PICKUP

All year The Bitter Drafter has been building his own war chest of free-agent dollars. But for far less noble reasons than The Hydra. He doesn't want to pick up a stud, or even hold a guy hostage in a trade. He simply wants to cause damage.

He's akin to what Donald Rumsfeld labeled the Iraqi Dead-Enders— a group of Baath Party loyalists who've been tossed out of power and are now content to scamper around in the back alleys, support the insurgency, plant some IEDs, and recruit Saudi Arabians for suicide missions.

Pointless. Wasteful. But annoyingly effective in knocking forward-leaning teams off their strides.

THE FECKLESS UN OBSERVATION PARTY PICKUP

There are always a number of team managers who never get around to finding players. They think about it and maybe read a few articles on NFL.com, but it seldom goes any further than that.

They're like a UN observation team that drops into Somalia to "investigate" and "monitor" local goings-on. They trot around with their light blue helmets and perhaps conduct some "exploratory" missions. But ultimately, they end up posting up at the Hilton and snacking on hummus and figs.

Each week Adam Goldman considers picking up a free agent, but he somehow never gets around to it. This is mostly because he's sidetracked by other demands. For one thing, he has neglected to find a rabbi for his wedding.

"Forget your stupid free-agent dollars, Adam," Margaret harangued earlier in the day. "I'm flying blind here. If you want me to Jew up this wedding to keep your mommy happy, then you'd better find a rabbi. Just make sure he's not one of those squirrelly types with the fake Eastern European accent."

"I gotcha. I'll get on the rabbi circuit." Adam started thumbing through a Manhattan rabbinical directory. As it turns out, it was a lot like selecting a doctor or a plumber.

But as for picking up new players, Goldman simply lacks focus. He tries halfheartedly to spread his dollars around. So he bids twelve dollars on Dallas Clark, fourteen on Amos Zereoue, and thirteen on Kerry Collins. But each time, his bid is turned down; his strategy has the same effect as sending food and medical supplies to various hot spots around the world.

Most of his efforts are wasted.

And eventually, Goldman realizes that it's best to avoid antagonizing the natives, stay out of trouble, and keep the peace.

Nothing to see here. Merely diplomacy in action.

THE BLACK GUY IN A HORROR MOVIE PICKUP

A black guy in a horror movie is usually kneecapped right out of the gate. He might have time to deliver a throwaway "Whatchoo talkin' about, Willis?" in the opening scene, but beyond that he's toast.

Sooner rather than later he'll be alone, sprinting through the forest, and will run headlong into a Jason Voorhees–Michael Myers meat grinder.

FIRST TEAM ALL-HORROR FILM SLASHERS

1. **Michael Myers**—once ate a dog
2. **Jason Voorhees**—underappreciated; the Tiki Barber of horror movies
3. **Freddie Krueger**—can make something out of nothing
4. **Leatherface**—showed that he still had skills in the remake of *The Texas Chainsaw Massacre*
5. **Pinhead**—"What you think of as pain is a shadow. Pain has a face. Allow me to show it to you. Gentlemen, I . . . am . . . pain."
6. **Norman Bates**—key sixth man; savvy veteran role player; Mr. Intangibles

In free agency the plot is often the same. A previously unknown player scores a big touchdown on Monday Night Football and does a scrappy backflip in the end zone. He's like Cuba Gooding Jr.[23] in *Jerry Maguire*. Only not annoying.

---

23. Has any Academy Award–winning actor done less after winning the award? He went from *Jerry Maguire* to *Snow Dogs*. Soon he'll be playing Goofy at Disneyland. Cuba Gooding Jr. is the Harold Minor of actors.

In the days that follow, this potential free-agent target rockets into the consciousness of fantasy football managers. But you know that it can't last. It's too good to be true. The guy is going down.

It's at this point that The Mick enters the picture. Despite his misanthropy, he loves a good story. And his latest free-agent conquest, Roy Williams—a rookie wide receiver for the ever-unreliable Detroit Lions—was on a tear the past few weeks.

"Stay healthy, young buck, just stay healthy," The Mick says.

The Mick inserts Williams into his starting lineup. He's expecting big things. But said things don't last more than three minutes and eight seconds into the second quarter before Williams gets whipsawed while plowing forward in a short yardage situation, and blows out his knee.

In horror movie terms Williams is high-stepping through the woods, he's looking back to check that the coast is clear, then he turns back around . . . and promptly runs straight into a machete.

O'Brien's stunned.

The text messages on his cell phone are instantaneous. It's as if the Bush League has stopped everything to watch The Mick's free agent get eviscerated.

"You're the Angel of Death, O'Brien," Schlots comments. *"Everything you touch meets a tragic end."*

"Can you let me know the next time you're in my neighborhood?" inquires Goldman. *"I'll be sure to mark my front door with lamb's blood."*

The Mick shakes his head, runs both his hands through his hair, and emits a silent scream.

THE LONG KISS GOOD-BYE DROP

While most managers concentrate on pickups, few consider the difficult choice of dropping players. Sure, cutting an injured player is easy. But what do you make of the veteran player who's slumping? Or the young gun who hasn't gotten his snaps?

Someone has to go. But nothing is more frustrating than cutting the wrong player, and nothing is more disheartening than seeing that same player experience success after being picked up a few weeks later by a mortal enemy.

The best thing to do is avoid regret. Once you drop a player, stop thinking about him. You should just wash your hands and move on.

When it comes to cutting talent, Donald Trump is our role model. He has no second thoughts when he flicks his annoying cobralike "Yuh fie-yahd" hand gesture at some whimpering "Apprentice" assclown. But Trump, despite being a complete phony, is a rarity. He's a cyborg, lacking any sort of genuine empathy.

TOP FIVE REALITY-TV ASS-CLOWNS

1. Omarosa, *The Apprentice*
2. Coral, *The Real World*
3. Puck, *The Real World*
4. Any person on *My Super Sweet 16*
5. Steven from *Laguna Beach*

The same can't be said for Kwame Jones, who's laced with regret every time he drops a player. This is because, as a former athlete, he respects "the brotherhood of ballers" and never likes letting anyone go.

"I need football players," Kwame says, "not football stars." If he could start Tedy Bruschi, Doug Flutie, and Eddie George—guys Howie Long refers to as "men's men"—Kwame would. But he can't. So he grumbles instead, and maintains a short leash on his guys.

The man is a football guy. He *understands* football. He's *played* football. But it's that genuine football knowledge that tends to upend him. Kwame goes south on a player quickly if the player has sloppy technique, lack of hustle, or poor preparation. Likewise, he puts a premium on guys who play through injuries.

So when his Domanick Davis starts running with a "hitch in his giddyup," Kwame's brow furrows. He strokes his chin and observes, "Mr. Davis doesn't seem to want the rock anymore."

Kwame then does the inexplicable. He drops his stud for Charlie Garner, who, in Kwame's estimation, is playing with a "renewed sense of urgency."

Whatever that means.

So out goes Davis, in comes Garner, and down go Kwame's chances for a championship season. Two weeks later Davis is back in strong form, darting around, scoring touchdowns.

For another Bush League team.

And the once-tempting Garner? He's back in a crippling running-back-by-committee with Mike Alstott and Michael Pittman.

Where he belongs.

"Kwame, perhaps it's me being a glass-is-half-empty guy, but I suspect you regret that decision to drop Domanick Davis," observes The Mick.

Kwame pinches the bridge of his nose and crinkles his lips. "Yes, a regrettable choice. I'm sorry that I disrespected a former member of my team."

Somewhere Mr. Trump purses his lips and mutters to himself, "Kwame, yuh fie-yahd."

OTHER FREE-AGENT PICKUPS

1. **The Cock-Block Pickup:** Manager acquires a player that he doesn't need but that a rival manager does
2. **The Napa Valley Pickup:** Manager secures a young, unproven player, hoping that he'll ripen in the second half of the season
3. **The One-Night-Stand Pickup:** Manager picks up player for a week, quickly realizes the player is a lemon, and drops him the following week
4. **The Arbitrage Pickup:** Player acquired for pure trade value
5. **The Rolling Thunder Pickup:** Manager acquires a different defense each week to exploit matchups

<< RAGE AGAINST >>
THE EXPERTS E-MAIL

THE BEAUTY OF FANTASY FOOTBALL IS THAT EVERYONE IS an "expert." Call yourself an analyst, write some columns on an obscure Web site, churn out voluminous postings on Internet message boards, and your legend spreads. Anyone can do it. (Hell, we're writing a book after all.)

The irony of all this is that fantasy managers still spend a tremendous amount of time reading the "expert" commentary. They can't help themselves.

They know that most of these experts know nothing more than they do. Yet there is a certain comfort in making decisions recommended by those in authority.

At a certain point in the season, however, someone snaps. Enough is enough. It's time to take a stand.

From:	The Bitter Drafter
Sent:	November 2, 2004
To:	Bush League Mailing List
Subject:	Rage Against the Experts

Can we have an open discussion about the dirty little secret that nobody likes to talk about? I'm referring to the "expert commentary" on the fantasy Web site du jour. I know that this is not a popular topic at most dinner parties, but I am just saying what everyone else is thinking. My view is that just like genital herpes, if we get it out into the open, we'll all learn a little something and maybe, just maybe, be the better for it.

There are two forms of commentary that I find particularly insidious: "mailbag questions" and "player analysis." Here are my primary gripes, how I would answer these silly questions, and how I would do things if I ran the world.

Gripe #1—The Mailbag: Impossible Scenario

Dear "Expert,"

I don't know who to start at QB this week. Peyton Manning is on a bye, and I have to choose between Daunte Culpepper and Donovan McNabb. What should I do?

—Roger W.

Dear Roger,

I suggest you ditch the two-person league that you are currently in with your little sister and join another league. Preferably one composed of males above the age of eleven. This should be easy for you, given that you are a registered sex offender and may have no other choice. Barring that, I would drop McNabb, pick up Joey Harrington (if he's still available), and ride that horse to victory.

Gripe #2—Player Analysis: Stating the Obvious

Torry Holt's consistency is legendary, and the fact that he's peaking is good news. Despite the matchup, you should start him against Philly.

But the Philly cornerbacks have catlike reflexes. I've got Reche Caldwell going up against the 49ers this week, and they've got a *terrible* pass defense. As long as Caldwell's surgically repaired knee holds up and he gets playing time, the man has tremendous sleeper potential. Besides, Torry could use the rest.

Gripe #3—Player Analysis: Inactionable Advice

Chris Brown now has three straight 100-yard games. He is quickly emerging as a solid number-two RB. If he is still available, grab him off waivers.

Tell you what, if he is still available, please light yourself on fire for not getting him two weeks ago. What's wrong with these people?

Maybe I'm being too harsh and they're trying to cater to leagues with six players or less.

That sort of stuff infuriates me, even when I'm medicated.

Gripe #4—The Mailbag: Softball Question

My league requires that we start two running backs, and I need to pick from the following four: Shaun Alexander, Ron Dayne, Deuce McAllister, and Ricky Watters. Who should I choose?

If I were your mother, I would have chosen birth control. Now, Ron Dayne was great in college. And Ricky Watters would have been a fine selection in 1999. But given that those facts are irrelevant, I would go with Shaun and Deuce. They are "stud" RBs and give you the best chance of winning.

Also, butt-wiping is more effective when done in an up-and-down motion versus the circular technique you currently use. So keep that in mind as well.

Gripe #5—Player Analysis: Unsubstantiated Claims

Tyrone Calico took off his knee brace for the first time this week. He is a nice sleeper candidate if he's still available.

Why? Is he Forrest Gump?

Or from this week . . .

Donald Driver is a must-start every week, but he should dominate vs. Minnesota in Week Four.

The fact that they even use the word "dominate" is a wart on the nose of journalistic objectivity. In other leagues I get turned down for trades because of this rubbish. Sure, I know Terrell Owens is a must-start every week, but can he *dominate* like Driver? Not according to the experts.

Gripe #6—Player Analysis: Backhanded Compliment

Brandon Lloyd is a decent number-three option for owners who need to replace a regular wide receiver on a bye.

What the hell is that supposed to mean? Could you insult the guy a little more? It's like saying a girl at the bar would be good-looking if you were blind, drunk, and had an hour to live.

Why not just say, "Brandon Lloyd really stinks, but hey, you're desperate and there's nobody else."

Actually, wait a minute, this is not a gripe. I like that answer. Especially when they write that someone has absolutely no fantasy value whatsoever and should never be picked under any circumstance, ever. I retract this gripe.

That is all. I'm done venting. Please, go about your business.

21

<< THE DEATH MAIDEN >> GRACES THE BUMP-N-RUN

"Hey, guys," Prash says, "I've invented a new nickname. Want to hear it?" He's met by a collective shrug. "It's Shooon—like the end of Prashun. Want to say it with me?"

"Dude," Schlots says. "You can't make up your own nickname."

"He's right," Goldman says. "Nicknames have to be bestowed upon you—you can't just give them to yourself."

"Sure you can. Look at P. Diddy."

"You're not P. Diddy. You're P. Thind."

"No, I'm Shoooooooon."

"Stop that," O'Brien says.

Prash cups his hands around his mouth. "Shhhhooooooooon."

O'Brien gets up.

"Shhhhhhhooooon."

O'Brien escapes to the bar.

"SHHHHHOOOOOOON."

ANNOYING SELF-APPOINTED NICKNAMES

1. Puff Daddy, P. Diddy, Puffy, and whatever Sean Combs comes up with next
2. The Artist Formerly Known as Prince
3. Brian "the Boz" Bosworth
4. Adam "Pacman" Jones
5. Rod "He Hate Me" Smart

ANNOYING NICKNAMES (GENERAL)

1. Deion "Prime Time" Sanders
2. Lou "The Toe" Groza
3. Lester "The Molestor" Hayes
4. Gary "The Glove" Payton
5. Eric "Butterbean" Eschy

12:59 P.M.

"Kwame is a no show," The Mick says. "What's the deal?"

"He called me earlier. He's stuck at his school," says Goldman. "He mentioned something about preparing for parent-teacher conferences."

"Wow. You gotta question his priorities. We may have an absentee commish on our hands."

"Maybe we should stage a coup," says Thind. "I could be the new commissioner. I'd usher in a new era—the reign of Shoon. I'd rule with an iron fist."

"There's nothing iron about your fist, Prashun," says Schlots. "Besides, Kwame is the best commish the Bush League has ever had."

"True, that," says Goldman. "He's the rock that keeps this league together."

1:12 P.M.

Kickoff in D.C. The Seahawks storm downfield. A camera flies overhead, and somewhere in this whirl of activity there's the amplified sound of violence—pads on pads, the grating of plastic. Prash looks a little stoned. "It's a video game," he says. "These days everything looks like a video game."

TOP TEN SPORTS VIDEO GAMES

1. **Madden NFL**—The Bentley of football games
2. **NBA Jam: Tournament Edition**—Responsible for hundreds of dollars spent during college; featured a variety of secret characters, the best of which was President Bill Clinton
3. **One on One: Dr. J vs. Larry Bird**—Introduced dunks, crowd noise, and shattering backboards
4. **FIFA Soccer**—The most popular sports video game in the world
5. **Wayne Gretzky NHL**—First video game to feature blood and injured players
6. **Pole Position**—Rocking the Fuji track was heavenly
7. **Punch Out**—Beating Glass Joe built confidence and self-esteem
8. **Golden Tee**—Groups of antisocial men hammer away at a round track ball, and take it seriously
9. **Tecmo Bowl**—The granddaddy of sports video games. If you ever played with Bo Jackson, you know what we mean
10. **Earl Weaver Baseball**—First game to have tons of historical stats

The Death Maiden makes a surprise appearance.

"Well, well, well," Thind says. "Look what the cat's dragged in."

"Death Maiden," Goldman says, "what are you doing here?"

"My husband's studying for the bar."

"Who? What?"

"I wanted to watch the games, but I had to leave my apartment."

"Wait," Thind says, "you're married?"

"I am." She shows her ring.

"I had no idea. Anyone else know that?"

"Nope."

"Death Maiden," Thind says, "we've been playing fantasy football with you for three years now, and you've never once mentioned your husband."

"You never asked."

"Good point," says Goldman.

"Hold on just a second," Thind says. "Is your husband uncomfortable with you hanging out in a bar with a bunch of dudes?"

"My husband is still active in the National Guard. If there were any problems, he'd probably just whip your asses."

"Fair point," Thind says.

"Makes sense to me," Schlots adds.

"Death Maiden," The Mick says, "at least you'll be able to watch the games with experts."

"Chris, I'm three games ahead of you."

"So?"

"I'm not sure that you're much of an expert."

Thind gets up and high-fives her. "Welcome to the show."

Daunte Culpepper airmails the ball eighty-five yards to a streaking Randy Moss. Moss removes his helmet, his Afro resembling a truffula tree from *The Lorax*.[24] Then Daunte does his little rumba dance, and Schlots gets up and mirrors his movements, his stomach jiggling as he dances.

3:54 P.M.

Thind's starting running backs score three touchdowns and run for 234 combined yards, earning him 42 points on the day. How do we know? Because Thind pulls out a Sharpie and does a "primitive calculation" on a cocktail napkin. He then finds a second cocktail napkin and "confirms" his score.[25]

4:13 P.M.

At the start of the Giants' game, safety Shaun Williams flubs an open-field tackle. "Jesus Christ, wrap up," The Death Maiden shouts. "Use your arms *and* your legs." There's a moment of silence before the table breaks out in a round of golf claps.

5:17 P.M.

Schlots hears the five-note CBS sports-ticker tune and comes bolting out of the bathroom, his belt still unbuckled. He watches closely as the top ten running backs of the day scroll across the bottom of the screen. Each running back is followed by his current stats for rushing, receiving, and touchdowns.

None of them are his.

"The last guy on the ticker has 52 yards," Goldman says.

"Saw that."

"None of your boys are on that list."

---

24. The Lorax is one of the most tragic figures in modern literature. Walrus-mustachioed and largely ignored, he endured the wrath of the Once-ler family, the face of modern industrialism: "But I had to grow bigger. So bigger I got. I biggered my factory. I biggered my roads. I biggered my wagons. I biggered the loads."

25. There's nothing more annoying in fantasy football than a manager who calculates his score on the fly. It's like the kid in high school who was too eager to show you his report card.

"Yup."

"So none of your backs have more than 52 yards, right?"

"Seems to be the case."

"Slow start, Schlots, slow start."

Schlots nods and quietly half-jogs back into the bathroom.

5:25 P.M.

Thind flags another Bumpette over. "What can I get you, hon?"

"Shoon, my name is Shooo—" The Bumpette flips her wrist, does a one-eighty, and beelines back to the bar.

5:33 P.M.

A Cleveland fan (aka "Big Dawg") stands up as Jeff Garcia scrambles, ducks under a defensive lineman, appears headed for a first down, and then slides two yards short. "Why, Lord?" Big Dawg says. "Why do I have to watch Garcia play each week?"

TOP FIVE QUARTERBACKS QUICKEST TO HOOK-SLIDE

1. Bernie Kosar
2. Steve DeBerg
3. Vinny Testaverde
4. Bubby Brister
5. Brad Johnson

6:13 P.M.

The Death Maiden gathers her stuff. "Boys, I've gotta run."

Thind autographs a cocktail napkin and gives it to her.

She smiles and places the napkin in her purse.

"You've been real cool," Schlots says. "It doesn't even seem like you're a girl." The Death Maiden frowns. "I mean that in a good way."

6:53 P.M.

The sun is setting through the cheap tinted windows at the front of the Bump-N-Run. "Another beautiful day," Goldman says. "And what did I do? I was in a bar. I spent all day in this dark, musty, disgusting bar with a bunch of dudes."

"And one chick," Thind says.

"What?"

"A bunch of dudes and one chick."

"Right. Still seems like a waste of a day."

"Hey, at least we learned something about The Death Maiden. How often does that happen?"

"Not often," Schlots says. "Plus, we learned that her husband's an ass-kicker. That's good for future reference."

22

<< SCHADENFREUDE >>

FROM TIME TO TIME WE ALL INDULGE IN "SCHADEN-
freude," a German word that literally means, "joy from damage."
We're constantly rooting for bad things to happen to other managers,
teams, and players.

A tweaked hamstring.

A dropped pass.

A botched trade.

Bad things—things that generate smiles, chuckles, and knowing nods.

But that doesn't make us cruel, exactly. It merely makes us good
fantasy managers. Because at the end of the day, in the world of fantasy football, schadenfreude is just another form of passion.

THE HIGH ANKLE SPRAIN—PULLING FOR AN INJURY

We'll admit it up front: We actively pull for injuries. In certain
cases, we hope and even pray that a player goes down with a torn ACL
(or the slightly more amusing "high ankle sprain"). And yes, it's
true—when they don't get up, we've even applauded.

To some, that might seem mean-spirited. The moral code of sports dictates that you should want to beat an opponent fair and square. Even if an injury helps your team, you shouldn't be happy about it, much less cheer.

Needless to say, this moral code does not apply to fantasy football. And it certainly does *not* apply to the Bush League, where all managers engage in schadenfreude. Even a classy guy like Kwame Jones roots for this sort of carnage.

AMUSING INJURIES

1. Groin Strain
2. Lateral Meniscus Tear
3. Neck Stinger
4. Buttocks Contusion
5. Hip Pointer

This week he's engaged in an intradivisional matchup with The Mick, who happens to be starting Clinton Portis. For most of the season Portis has been underperforming, but now he seems to have found his groove. Any fantasy manager worth his salt knows that Portis is a constant threat to break a 50-yarder, and The Mick's constant reminders of this fact aren't helping matters any.

So Kwame clamps down, closes his eyes, and thinks, *God, I'd love to see Portis tweak his groin.* And then it hits. Just what the doctor ordered. Portis pulls up lame. He's either a pulled hamstring or is cramping severely. Either way, Portis hobbles off to the sidelines.

He won't be seeing action again anytime soon.

It's a moment of pure bliss.

"Bad break, O'Brien," says Kwame. "Bad. Break."

"Fuck. You. Twice."

FOXSports shows Portis bent over on the sidelines. His hands are on his knees and he's shaking his head. And as good a guy as Kwame is, he doesn't mind this image. No, he doesn't mind it at all.

F*&$ DUKE—PULLING FOR AN UNLIKELY UPSET

Each year we go to Vegas for the opening weekend of March Madness. We spend most of our days inside the Mandalay Bay sports book, where we bet on fourteen and fifteen seeds to upset two or three seeds, because they're underdogs, and they usually have pasty, malnourished-seeming point guards who specialize in "hustle" plays.

But if we're being truly honest, in most instances we're simply rooting *against* powerhouses. And, more specifically, against their fans. Because few things in life are more satisfying than watching a Kansas fan (decked out in shiny Jayhawks gear) cramp up as his squad full of McDonald's All-Americans chokes against Southwest Missouri State.

And there's nothing—absolutely nothing—more satisfying than watching Duke lose while sitting near a Blue Devils fan who's bragged to anyone and everyone within earshot about Grant Hill's "insane" dunk or Trajan Langdon's "sweet stroke."

Duke fans are sanctimonious and terrible people. In most cases we'd rather watch them lose than watch our own teams win. (For some reason we felt especially this way about the Blue Devil squads led by Chris Collins and Steve "Wojo" Wojciechowski, the originators of the white-guys-signaling-that-they'll-play-tough-defense-by-slapping-the-floor move.)

MOST-ANNOYING BLUE DEVILS

1. Christian Laettner
2. Bobby Hurley
3. Steve "Wojo" Wojciechowski
4. Chris Collins
5. Danny Ferry
6. J. J. Redick
7. Quinn Snyder
8. Cherokee Parks
9. Thomas Hill
10. Alaa Abdelnaby

This sort of thinking carries over to fantasy football as well. Once Bush League managers fall out of title contention, we start spending energy hoping that great teams run by annoying managers suffer soul-crippling losses.

So when the relentlessly ineffective Two-Headed Hydra beats the Thindianapolis Colts on six field goals from David Akers and an interception returned for a touchdown from the Jaguars defense, all Bush League managers start doing *Saturday Night Fever* dances.

All managers, that is, except Prashun Thind, who called his second loss of the season "unreal," "upsetting," and "contrary to the natural order of things." We know how Thind feels—getting beaten by a scrap-heap team is like losing an "all-in" Poker hand on the flop, and then having Phil Gordon tell you that the odds were ninety-eight to one in your favor.

And that makes his defeat even more amusing.

"Good form, Hydra," says Kwame. "Well executed."

"We're calling you 'Giant Killer' from now on," says Schlots.

"That even made *me* smile," adds The Bitter Drafter.

"Thanks, guys!" Hydra says. "I think we're finally getting the hang of this."

"No," Schlots says, "you're not—you just bumped off a really annoying team, and that makes you king for the day."

"We'll take it!"

"You guys are just happy because your teams are out of the running and my squad is still dominant," Thind says. "You shouldn't player-hate, homies."

Perhaps Thind has a point. But in this moment, we're enjoying watching him get his ankle kicked once or twice. Much of this schadenfreude has been building up all year because Thind has an annoyingly effective team and no humility. Which makes it all that much sweeter to watch him go down. Just like every great Duke loss.

A DIANE CHAMBERS KICK IN THE BALLS— PULLING AGAINST A TRADED PLAYER

Injuries, tough matchups, and rotten luck can contribute to a losing season. But a bad trade? Well, that's all on you.

You're the sucker who traded an Air Jordan rookie card to your older brother for a sheet of rub-on tattoos. You're the jackass who dumped the cute-but-quiet Lisa in ninth grade to date Lily, the "mannish" slam poetry chick. A year later Lisa became the homecoming queen. Lily, meanwhile, remained mannish and tended to shout unnecessarily. You curse Lisa, pretty though she may be, as the one who got away.

This sort of thing can engender bitterness and hostility. You start to hate what you've given up, which reminds us of a classic exchange on *Cheers* between Sam Malone and Diane Chambers:

> **Sam:** And while you're up there floating around, remember the day I said this: You are the nuttiest, the stupidest, the phoniest fruitcake I ever met.

Diane: You, Sam Malone, are the most arrogant, self-centered son of a—

Sam: SHUT UP. Shut your fat mouth.

Diane: Make me.

Sam: Make you? My God, I'm gonna . . . I'm gonna . . . I'm gonna bounce you off every wall of this office.

Diane: Try it and you'll be walking funny tomorrow. Or should I say funnier.

There are several great aspects to this exchange. The first is Sam saying "phoniest fruitcake." We never tire of this phrase, and wish that it were used more often. Second, we appreciate the threat—from an iconic sitcom character no less—to engage in first-degree assault on a woman. Curious message. Third, any time a woman threatens to kick a guy in the balls, it's funny.

Arguably uncalled for, but funny.

But what drove this interaction? Ultimately, Sam's rage is driven by Diane's decision to date another man. He's frustrated and mad at himself. So he lashes out.

Such a phenomenon happens in fantasy football as well. Once you've traded a player, even if you loved him when he was on your team, you wish him nothing but ill will in his new environment.

Al Lopez drafted Corey Dillon, and for eight weeks he cheered for him. "If Corey came to Casa Lopez," he exclaimed one Sunday, "I'd make him my special fajitas with mango sauce. And for desert I'd give him nothing but Ben & Jerry's."

All of this held true . . . until Lopez, needing to shake up his team, traded Dillon and Andre Johnson for Shaun Alexander and assorted riffraff.

"Must have been tough letting Dillon go," Thind says.

"He's dead to me," Lopez responds.

"But he was your boy. You cheered for him each and every Sunday."

"I hope he never gains another yard."

"What about catches?"

"No catches, no yards, no touchdowns."

"Seems harsh."

"That's the way the cookie crumbles, Thind."

In Bush League trades, it's not enough to enjoy your new players; you must also wish that those who've left your team are suffering, and suffering badly. After all, losing a player who goes on to help another man is really no better than a Diane Chambers kick in the balls.

BLEEDING IT OUT—PULLING AGAINST YOUR OWN PLAYER

Say you draft a promising young running back in the fourth round. He's supposed to be your second running back. But from week one he has underperformed, and now he's riding the pine next to Freddie Mitchell.[26]

This player is a disgrace. He's failed your team, insulted your honor, and made you the laughingstock of the league. Now you simply want him to perform miserably, and fall on his sword—ready to be cut.

It's the right thing to do. A model for doing the "right thing" can be found in *The Godfather Part II* when Tom Hagen chats with the jailed witness, Frank Pentangeli:

> **Tom Hagen:** When a plot against the emperor failed . . . the plotters were always given a chance . . . to let their families keep their fortunes. Right?
>
> **Frank Pentangeli:** Yeah, but only the rich guys, Tom. The little guys got knocked off and all their estates went to the

---

26. There's no player in the NFL more annoying than Freddie Mitchell. This is a guy who gave himself multiple nicknames—FredEx, The People's Champ, and The Sultan of Slot—but talked more than he played.

emperors. Unless they went home and killed themselves, then nothing happened. And the families . . . the families were taken care of.

Tom Hagen: That was a good break. A nice deal.

The Mick, who has been burned many times by bench players going off at the end of the year, is the primary purveyor of bleeding-it-out schadenfreude. He wants his players to take a "nice deal." And this season has been no exception. The Mick started Kevin Jones for the first three weeks before benching him.

But lately Jones has heated up.

Many managers would be excited to see a player's promise fulfilled in the latter weeks of a season. But not The Mick. In his mind Jones has betrayed the family. *"He should do the honorable thing and simply disappear. Bleed himself out in a bathtub. I don't ever want to see his name in a box score again."*

Unfortunately, Jones does not heed The Mick's demands. No, he continues to rally in a big way—rattling off a series of strong games in weeks ten and eleven. The Mick should start him, but he refuses to budge.

"I just don't trust him," he writes. *"Each good game should be his last."*

"Kevin Jones sure looks good on your bench," Schlots replies, adding a *"☺"* for full effect. *"If you're not using him, I'll take him off your hands."*

"Kevin Jones is falling on his sword."

"What?"

"I said, Kevin Jones . . . must . . . fall . . . on . . . his . . . sword."

"Geez, Mick, lighten up, man."

The Mick grinds his teeth and contemplates the likelihood of a serious injury befalling Schlots. Or Kevin Jones. Or getting arrested for pistol-whipping a Safeway checkout boy.

All a bit too complicated, concedes The Mick. Why couldn't Kevin Jones have just done the honorable thing and bled himself out?

SKELETOR AND THE LONELINESS OF EVIL—PULLING AGAINST A COACH

Make no bones about it: There's a conflict of interest between NFL coaches and fantasy managers. A coach cares about winning, whereas a fantasy manager is indifferent to team results, opting instead to focus on starts, injury reports, and red-zone touches.

A fantasy football manager doesn't even particularly care if a coach does his job well. He just wants accurate information and consistent strategies. Don't hide player injuries. Don't rotate running backs. And for God's sake, don't throw random passes to tight ends inside the five.

Mike Shanahan, this means you.

Please pay attention.

Coach Shanahan, aka "Skeletor," might be the most hated coach in fantasy football. Year after year, he creates devastating fantasy offenses. And year after year, he creates unbelievable amounts of ambiguity around said offenses.

TOP "MASTERS OF THE UNIVERSE" CHARACTERS

1. He-Man
2. Skeletor
3. Man-at-Arms
4. Ram Man
5. Stinkor
6. Clawful
7. Two-Bad
8. Twistoid
9. Scare Glow
10. Ninjor

It's entirely possible that in real life Coach Shanahan is a wonderful human being. But in the realm of fantasy football, Shanahan is pure evil—a trait he shares with his alter ego:

> **Skeletor:** Tell me about the loneliness of good, He-Man. Is it equal to the loneliness of evil?

Shanahan's basic crime is that he's shifty and cagey (or possibly cagey and shifty) in announcing his starting lineup. This is particularly the case with his stable of running backs, all of whom are capable of wracking up 100-yard games and scoring multiple touchdowns.

He does this, apparently, to keep opposing coaches off balance. And while this might be a successful strategy in the NFL, it's absolutely irritating to fantasy football managers attempting to decide between Mike Anderson, Terrell Davis, Clinton Portis, Quentin Griffin, Tatum Bell, or, heaven forbid, Maurice Clarett.

Coach Shanahan also likes to run an unpredictable offense. A naked bootleg for Jake Plummer. A short screen pass to Patrick Hape. Jeb Putzier on a fly pattern. Skeletor has called all of these plays in the red zone when he should have just handed off the ball to his unstoppable running back du jour. And this play-calling cripples fantasy football managers.

Coach Shanahan is the target of ruthless schadenfreude—from seeing his teams get routed by Kansas City and San Diego, to Jake Plummer scrambling and throwing a left-handed interception, to those amusing icicles that form under his nose during particularly cold mile-high conditions.

Let him suffer.

And despite it all we're pretty sure that Coach Shanahan doesn't much care about the fantasy football goons who curse his name. He's Skeletor, after all, a man who shows no remorse:

> **He-Man:** You promised not to hurt them!
> **Skeletor:** I lied.

DANTE'S NINTH CIRCLE OF HELL—PULLING AGAINST YOUR HOMETOWN TEAM

Adam Goldman is a loyal fellow. He's never cheated on his fiancée. He calls his parents every Saturday. And he has always—*always*—rooted for the Giants.

But now he's facing a "great unpleasantness." His stud wide receiver, Terrell Owens, is going up against the paper-thin New York secondary. A big day for TO is undoubtedly a rough day for the Giants.

What to do, what to do?

As it turns out, his decision is as twisted as a pretzel. Adam roots relentlessly for Owens to break every catch for a long gainer, but wants the Giants to "stay in the game." And when he's caught cheering for the Eagles—the Eagles!—by his fellow Bush League managers, he just smiles sheepishly and says, "Well, the Giants suck balls anyhow. If TO eats them alive, we'll have a better draft pick, and that will lead to a dynasty again, and—"

"Adam," Schlots interrupts, "how can you root against your beloved Giants?"

"Well, I'm not really rooting *against* the Giants."

"You're not?"

"No, I'm rooting *for* TO. There's a difference."

"There is?"

"Yeah, I think so."

"I don't know—I can't imagine rooting against Notre Dame under any circumstance."

"This is different—I'm still a Giants fan; I just want TO to get his yards."

Schlots scratches his head. "Nope, I'm sorry," he says. "That won't work. It's sinful what you're doing, Adam. Just sinful."

23

<< MEN BEHAVING BADLY >>

SOMETIMES THE BUSH LEAGUE COMMUNITY DETOURS away from fantasy football and devolves into meaningless guy banter. This tends to happen in late November, when managers who are clearly out of contention turn their attention to acts of naked verbal aggression.

It's the game within the game, and it can be taken too far. The following e-mail chain started innocently enough but, in standard form, spiraled out of control rather quickly.

That's how the Bush League rolls.

From: Lopez, Alejandro
Sent: Tuesday, November 23, 2004 9:53 PM
To: The Bush League
Subject: Bringing the Pain

The Cuban Missile Crisis is fired up about its latest trade. Make way for El Matador!

I hope you guys are all bundling up for your frigid New York winter. I, however, will be chilling here in LA, making secret deals, and raping you all.

From: O'Brien, Chris
Sent: Tuesday, November 23, 2004 10:01 PM
To: Alejandro Lopez
CC: The Bush League
Subject: Re: Bringing the Pain

Al:

Small point—I know that we're all in this for laughs and chuckles.

But, as someone who's had a family member who's been the victim of sexual assault, I ask that you refrain from using words like "rape" as a joke.

It's just a bit hard to swallow.

Thanks guys,

The Mick

From: Lopez, Alejandro
Sent: Tuesday, November 23, 2004 10:08 PM
To: O'Brien, Chris
CC: The Bush League
Subject: Re: Bringing the Pain

My apologies. I too have a similar situation. Didn't mean to offend.

From: Lopez, Alejandro
Sent: Tuesday, November 23, 2004 10:08 PM
To: Adam Goldman
Subject: Re: Bringing the Pain

Is this jagoff serious? I really can't tell.

From: Goldman, Adam
Sent: Tuesday, November 23, 2004 10:12 PM
To: Alejandro Lopez
Subject: Re: Bringing the Pain

My gut reaction when I read his initial response was that he was joking.

I've never heard anything about that from him—not that he'd necessarily talk about it. The Mick is about the last person in this entire league that should be offended by something said.

Either way, I wouldn't sweat it. Your apology, as far as I'm concerned, was a sign of weakness.

From: O'Brien, Chris
Sent: Tuesday, November 23, 2004 10:12 PM
To: Alejandro Lopez
Subject: Re: Bringing the Pain

You know that I was just fucking with you, right?

From: Lopez, Alejandro
Sent: Tuesday, November 23, 2004 10:15 PM
To: Chris O'Brien
Subject: Re: Bringing the Pain

Asshole. You made my heart drop into the pit of my stomach. I'll never take you seriously again.

From: Goldman, Adam
Sent: Tuesday, November 23, 2004 10:20 PM
To: Alejandro Lopez
Subject: Re: Bringing the Pain

So, did you get to the bottom of this yet?
I suspect you've been duped.

From: Lopez, Alejandro
Sent: Tuesday, November 23, 2004 10:23 PM
To: Adam Goldman
Subject: Re: Bringing the Pain

Just got an e-mail from him. He was fucking with me.
What an ass.

From: Goldman, Adam
Sent: Tuesday, November 23, 2004 10:25 PM
To: Alejandro Lopez
Subject: Re: Bringing the Pain

Ah yes, there you go. Knew my instincts were right.
What a jackass.

From: Lopez, Alejandro
Sent: Tuesday, November 23, 2004 10:26 PM
To: Adam Goldman
Subject: Re: Bringing the Pain

He's an asshole, and he'll pay.

From: Thind, Prashun
Sent: Tuesday, November 23, 2004 10:28 PM
To: Alejandro Lopez
CC: The Bush League
Subject: Re: Bringing the Pain

If it's not too much to ask, I wonder if you fags could settle down and focus on your wayward teams. Your little verbal food fight has grown tiresome.

From: Lopez, Alejandro
Sent: Tuesday, November 23, 2004 10:30 PM
To: Prashun Thind
CC: The Bush League
Subject: Re: Bringing the Pain

Prashun:
Small point. I know we're in this for fun and laughs, but can you refrain from using the word "fag"? I have a friend who used to be gay. His name is Chris O'Brien, and that derogatory term is a little hard to stomach for those of us who have been around gay people like him.
Thanks.

From: Thind, Prashun
Sent: Tuesday, November 23, 2004 10:33 PM
To: The Bush League
Subject: Re: Bringing the Pain

Fags, rape. What's next—hookers?

From: Schlotterbeck, John
Sent: Tuesday, November 23, 2004 10:35 PM
To: The Bush League
Subject: Re: Bringing the Pain

Me like hookers.

But enough about that, we have some fantasy football to play. Sunday is nearly upon us. And I'm already tasting chicken wings.

As an aside, a preemptive apology if my use of the word "hooker" offends anyone. I too have known hookers in my life, so I can empathize and sympathize.

Mmmmm. Chicken wings.

24

<< LATE-SEASON >>
REFLECTIONS

EARLY DECEMBER IS A TIME FOR REFLECTION. THE END OF
the season is fast approaching, and it's time to take stock.

Bush League managers start acting like senior citizens. Some
approach their teams with renewed vigor, hoping to squeeze every last
opportunity out of the season. Some managers have given in to
fatigue: They sleep more often, slurp chicken soup, and generally
tune out. And others simply get crotchety; they complain about how
their teams (or family) have failed them, the weather (in Green Bay),
and their arthritic hands (from overusing the remote).

All roads point to the great unknown—to the off-season. To life
beyond fantasy football. Yet it wasn't so long ago that the season had
just started. Oh, well. There's still time for final thoughts.

THE NIGERIAN NIGHTMARE REFLECTION

There comes a point in every season when a former champion realizes that this won't be his year. His team is fading fast from contention. And he has too much pride to scramble for a lowly wild-card
play-off spot.

Instead he starts comparing current front-runners to his old dynasty. And this comparison is rarely favorable. The new darlings of the Bush League have survived on flash and luck, but have little substance. Or so the former champion tells himself.

By mid-December, Al Lopez is out of the running. But rather than admit that he's simply had a bad season, his gut reaction is to blast the current front-runners. So when Goldman comments that Prash is "on a serious roll this year," he's met with disdain: "Forget it. Prash could never have won the league during the golden years."

"The golden years? Was the league really that different when you won?"

"Sure. Everyone tried. Every game counted."

"But Prash has only lost three games—"

"He would have lost eight during my run."

"He would have?"

"Of course. Those were harder times. The Bush League has gotten soft. It's no longer a league of sharks. We never used to have do-nothings like The Two-Headed Hydra."

"But . . . then why is your team 7–6?"

Lopez goes silent for a moment. "It isn't like the old days, I'll tell you that. We used to have backs that ran between the tackles. Guys like the 'Nigerian Nightmare' (aka Christian Okoye), Thurman Thomas, Ricky Watters, Icky Woods, and Roger Craig."

STUDLY FANTASY YEARS

1. **Marcus Allen, 1985.** 2,300 yards and 14 touches. But in his final twelve seasons he never had more than 1,150 combined yards
2. **Eric Dickerson, 1984.** 2,244 rushing yards and 14 touches. Just off Allen's best year
3. **John Riggins, 1983.** Alstott on steroids: 1,347 yards, 24 touches
4. **Walter Payton.** Mister consistency—ten years of at least 1,600 combined yards
5. **Jim Brown, 1965.** 1,872 yards and 21 touches during his final year in the league

"But, Al, we weren't even playing fantasy football then—"

"Here's what I know," Lopez says with some finality. "I know that Prash's team would never, ever have won the Bush League during the golden years. He simply does not have the mental makeup of an old-school team. That's not who he is. And if he wins the Bush League this year, it'll be hard to even consider it a *real* victory."

"Oh? What would you call it?"

Lopez hums. "A consolation prize for a stat geek."

"But not a ring? Not a title?"

"No, not a ring, and not a title."

The (former) champ has spoken. And so it goes: Nothing compares to the golden days, when the giants ruled the midway.

LANCE ARMSTRONG AND THE CHEATING DEATH REFLECTION

Many cancer survivors view life from a different, healthier perspective. They've faced their own mortality, they've accepted that they've been given a gift, and now they'll try with all their heart to enjoy what God has given them.

No person is a better example of this positive rebirth than Lance Armstrong. Ditched by his team, bedridden for months, given little hope—Lance fought back. And then he went on to bag a bunch of yellow jerseys and Sheryl Crowe. All and all, not a bad effort for a guy with one testicle and a prognosis of having two months to live.

The fantasy football equivalent (and admittedly we're being liberal here in our analogy) is the manager who comes back from a pathetic start to find himself in contention for a play-off spot. Such is the path taken by both Kwame and Schlots this year.

Kwame started 2–4, and things looked rather grim.

"Get yourself a shovel," The Mick said, "and dig six feet deep."

"Kwame Jones, Inc., never quits."

"Go on. Quit. Do it."

"Not going to happen."

Likewise, Schlots cobbled together his array of peculiar players and was initially written off.

"Schlots," Lopez said, "we've had this conversation before. I cannot see how The Fat Minnesota Guys manage to have a good season with your odd assortment of football castoffs."

"If I've said this once, I've said it a thousand times: The Fat Minnesota Guys have everything under control. This is all part of the plan."

Schlots's team staggered out of the gates initially. Like Kwame, he started 2–4, but now, through hard work, persistence, and a lucky break or two, both Kwame and Schlots have managed to go 7–1 the rest of the way, and they need just one more win to secure a play-off spot.

For some managers, a combined 8–5 record wouldn't excite them. But Kwame and Schlots feel as though they've been given a second chance. "My team has fought through adversity," Kwame tells the rest of the Bush League. "We love life. We love winning. It's all good."

"I toast the noble actions of Kwame Jones, Inc., and toast the great football spirit in the sky," says Schlots. "The Fat Minnesota Guys, like John Travolta in *Pulp Fiction*, are back from obscurity, having executed our strategy perfectly."

Both Kwame and Schlots have been given a new lease on their fantasy lives, and they don't intend to squander it.

REFLECTIONS OF THE MAD MEN

Let's face it: Some old men are simply unpleasant to be around. No matter the position of their wheelchairs, they're never facing the sun. No matter what food is prepared by the hospital, it's always too mushy. And when the grandkids visit, they'll swipe at them with a walking cane.

Some fantasy managers are the same way.

As the end nears, they eschew any pretense that fantasy football should be fun, focusing instead on being generally unpleasant to those around them. They lash out against lazy NFL players who have "quit" on them. They lash out at family members who won't let them "watch the game in peace." And they lash out at fellow Bush League managers.

This occurs most frequently when they're facing other lousy teams. If they were facing a good squad run by a respectable manager, they probably couldn't even be bothered to set their lineups. But throw two junkyard dogs into the same ring, and it's on.

In Week Thirteen The Mick (5–7) faces The Bitter Drafter (4–8), and all sense of decency goes out the window. It's like when Randy "Macho Man" Savage went up against Jake "The Snake" Roberts in the definitive villain vs. villain showdown. No one knew who to cheer for, but everyone knew bad things were coming.

To start things off The Mick calls The Bitter Drafter a "total waste of space," and The Bitter Drafter responds that The Mick is "a vile and duplicitous individual." The Mick then fires back that he doesn't "understand The Bitter Drafter's ten-cent words."

From there things further escalate.

The Mick says, "I'm going to boil your kids."

The Bitter Drafter says, "With your talent, you couldn't boil water."

"I'll boil your ass."

"I'll eat your boiled ass."

There's nothing particularly original here. Nothing clever to be parsed. No subtlety. These guys are running on fumes, and they know it.

"Guys," Kwame says, "let's try to end the year on a positive note, okay?"

"Sorry, Kwame," The Mick says, "that won't work for me."

"Me neither."

"I'm going to take this guy down if it's the last thing I do."

"Look, Kwame—this guy won't stop e-mailing me," The Bitter Drafter replies. "It's a crime. In fact, I'm considering filing a complaint."

"Let's keep this in perspective," says Kwame. "You're both under .500."

"So?" The Mick says.

"So, what does it matter if you're 6–7 or 5–8?"

There's a long silence before The Mick says, "I've got nothing left to play for, and I can't stand this guy. As I said before, I'm going to boil his ass."

Vaguely annoyed, and realizing that this conversation will never end, Kwame says, "Keep it to yourselves or you'll both be forfeiting."

There's moaning, and a few swipes at Kwame for "not listening," but after a while The Mick and The Bitter Drafter trail off. At this stage they're lacking energy, and there's only so much complaining that can be done.

THE LONG ISLAND INVESTMENT BANKER REFLECTION

A league leader is in a precarious position. On the one hand, the end of the season should be a celebration. His team rocks, and he's found success—so why shouldn't he kick back, puff on a cigar, and party like it's 1999? But on the other hand, his success has put him in a position where everything matters. How painful would it be if he lost the league title on one dopey move?

Free-agent acquisitions must be covered.

Trades must be made to block division rivals.

Starting lineups must be diligently monitored.

The league leader has a big responsibility, in short, to remain the league leader, even though at this point in the season he has a tremendous advantage over most other managers.

Consider a Wall Street investment banker who retires in his fifties.

Sure, he could head out to the country club and knock back a few gimlets—but in the back of his mind he knows that he could and probably should still be doing deals. He's still competitive, so he can't help but dabble and take a risk here or there.

Thind has three of the top seven running backs in the Bush League. He has two All-Pro wide receivers. His *backup* quarterback just had a forty-point game.

The Two-Headed Hydra could run his team and he'd still be in decent shape.

But that doesn't stop Prash from worrying. Each week, as he goes to the Bump-N-Run, he runs through his lineup just to confirm that there's no weak spot. He even fires in a trade to get *another* wide receiver just in case one of his guys goes down (and, at the same time, he strengthens the squad going up against Al Lopez—always satisfying).

"God, Prash, you'd think you were running a .500 team," says Schlots.

"I treat each week like I'm 0–0."

"But . . . you're 10–3."

"You can never be too prepared."

"But aren't you even enjoying your run to the title? Last year I was having a ball at this point in the season."

"Oh, I'm enjoying it," Prash says, smiling. "I'm having the time of my life. And this is how I do it. This is how I'm having fun."

CALLING DR. KEVORKIAN

Even if your team is lousy, basic decency requires that you finish out the season. You should try to make free-agent pickups and trades. You should notice when your team is on bye weeks. You should always set your starters. You should continue to participate so that the league maintains some competitive balance.

You should, but you don't.

Goldman, we're talking to you.

Kwame has been setting your starting lineup for the last three weeks. And you haven't even said thanks.

That's pathetic. You have called Dr. Kevorkian and decided to shut it down. You value your team no longer. In short: You've taken your final knee.

<< THE DAWNING OF >>
THE PLAY-OFFS E-MAIL

From: Thind, Prashun
Sent: Wednesday, December 15, 2004 1:23 PM
To: The Bush League
Subject: Play-offs, I say

Homeslices:

Every beginning has an end. For most of you the end is nigh.

If you must, for symbolic purposes only, make your final trade—Dorsey Levens for Sammy Morris comes to mind. (Question: What *does* make Sammy run?) Set your lineups against a nameless, shapeless opponent. Drop the Browns defense and add the 49ers instead.

Then shuffle off. Move along.

And for the four teams who made the play-offs—congrats. The dream lives on. Until you run into a buzz saw named the Thindianapolis Colts. And then your dream will die. Quickly.

Per tradition I present a quick breakdown on the final Bush League standings (broken down by our original draft order). As before, I neglected to mention certain managers entirely, due to your uninspired performances.

For those who *do* merit Thindy Infante's praise, enjoy this time. Bask in it. For you will shortly meet your maker.

So bring it. Bring. It. One last time.
Prashun Thind, League Scribe

#1 - Adam Goldman: The good news for Herr Doktor: He's getting married to (cue gong) the notorious Margaret Ming. The bad news? His team stunk. But Adam didn't make a nuisance of himself, ranting and raving about his team. He knew Team Goyim didn't have the goods to get it done, and he did the right thing. He took a knee. *No play-offs for you.*

#2 - Prash: Make way for the Road Warrior. Out of the barren desert has emerged a battle-tested, nasty challenger to the powers-that-be (and Tina Turner), and his name is . . . Thindy Infante. Riding on the back of grizzled veteran Curtis Martin, the Thindianapolis Colts have returned to the Promised Land. We have the most victories. We've scored the most points. Our power ranking is tops. And we . . . will . . . not . . . be . . . denied. *See you in the play-offs.*

#4 - Kwame Jones: Slow, meticulous, and boring—Kwame Jones, Inc., chugged along with little fanfare this season. But lo and behold, he's cobbled together a workmanlike 9–5 record. Look for him to bow out in the semifinals with grace and class. What a pussy. *See you in the play-offs.*

#6 - Schlots: Here's a funny one: Schlots is in the play-offs. His team full of hardscrabble journeymen perhaps mirrors his own upbringing, but that's no excuse. The Fat Minnesota Guys are just plain lousy. The guy still finds a way to start his crown jewel, James Mungro, for chrissakes. Yet there they are, rope-a-doping their way to a division title. These guys won two games by half a point each, for gawd's sake. It offends me to say this, but . . . *See you in the play-offs.*

#7 - The Bitter Drafter: By all accounts The Bitter Drafter had his most successful campaign to date: He pissed off eight different Bush League managers, sabotaged four different trades, picked up six different free agents he did not need, and . . . lost ten of his fourteen games. Carry on, Bitter Drafter. You loathsome, loathsome man. *No play-offs for you.*

#9 - The Death Maiden: I just threw up in my mouth as I prepared to type this, but it appears our female interloper, The Death Maiden, has reeled off *another* lucky/strong season. It's hard to explain how she did it. I suppose her fancy quarterback, Tom Brady, helped a bit. ("He's cute.") Some suggest she takes her fantasy football seriously, and has been good for some time. Thindy Infante has a hard time accepting that. Can't believe I'm saying this, but . . . *See you in the play-offs.*

#10 - El Matador: Father Time has clotheslined old Al. The once proud Aztec warrior, a perennial Bush League contender, has at last put down his sword and shield. No more clever drafting, no more savvy trading. Like his aging star, Brett Favre, the El Matador Express has run out of steam. It's getting a bit smelly in here. Think it's time to change baby Oscar's diapers. *No play-offs for you.*

#11—The Mick: His roster looked like a Jackson Pollock painting. Spotty, messy, and lined with random streaks of color. The Mick just never seemed to settle on a core roster. Schizophrenic. Always shifting players. Erratic and ill tempered. On the plus side, I hear that The Mick and his work colleague Venu Javarappa won "Product Management Team" of the year for their work on e-commerce solutions. I'm not sure how that's relevant. I just enjoy typing "e-commerce solutions" and "Venu Javarappa" in the same sentence. But as I was saying . . . *No play-offs for you.*

#12 - The Two-Headed Hydra: Honestly, I'm shocked these clowns won three games. They were the team that everyone circled on their schedules and penciled in as a win. Naturally they managed to deal the Thindianapolis Colts one of their few losses. But the Colts' one weakness is a tendency to play down to their opponent's level. In this case said level was rather low. *No play-offs for you.*

26

SCENES FROM A << WEDDING, AND THE >> PLAY-OFFS

12:12 P.M.

Adam sits quietly in the stretch limo en route to his wedding. Everything is happening in slow motion. His parents and the Mings accompany him in the limo. Mrs. Goldman is talking away, commenting on the tightness of her dress, and her displeasure with the flower arrangements. Adam starts to get nervous.

12:23 P.M.

Several Bush League members mill around the pre-wedding reception. They are handed yarmulkes and reluctantly put them on. Schlots comments that this all seems "a bit Jew-ey."

12:26 P.M.

Kwame sidles up to the group, chanting "Play-offs! Play-offs! Play-offs!" The play-off-bound Bush Leaguers exchange high fives. There is mutual respect among the "last men standing."

Kwame is facing The Death Maiden in one play-off match.

Thind and Schlots face off in the other.

"Been a good season, fellas," says Kwame. "We are the elite of the Bush League. Bask in the glory that is the play-offs."

Thind and Schlots do a quick jumping chest bump. Thind, upon contact, staggers back and stumbles into a waiter serving refreshments. Other guests look on with a mixture of bemusement and disdain.

12:36 P.M.

Thind does his first official breakdown of the day's upcoming play-off matchup. He faces Schlots, and, as usual, he's feeling very confident. Earlier that morning Thind printed out his and Schlots's rosters. Since his arrival at the wedding, he has been poring over the rosters, comparing players, identifying advantages.

"Schlots, I have to tell you. I've looked at our rosters, and I think I have you beat at every position. You may have an edge with your kicking unit. But that's about it," notes Thind.

"Games are won with special teams, Prash."

"Not in fantasy football."

"Don't worry about it, Thindy Infante. I also got my boy Rueben, and Rueben brings passion to my team."

"I don't get it. How is Rueben passionate?"

"His name is Rueben. Guys named Rueben are bringing it."

"Bringing what?"

"The heat, man."

"Christ, I hope we can sneak out and watch the afternoon games."

"Was thinking about that too."

"Would it be tacky?"

"Not if we're stealthy. Worst-case scenario, we take turns."

"I can't miss football this week. Not for a stupid wedding."

"We won't let that happen, Thind. Rueben needs me."

12:52 P.M.

Goldman walks through the crowd before joining the wedding party. He's sweating bullets. Adam shakes some hands, but seems to be out of breath. The Mick approaches him, and claps him on the back. "Let's keep this short, boyo. We got games to watch." Adam is not sure whether he's joking or serious. The Mick gives him a wink, and tells him to "break a leg."

12:53 P.M.

Schlots asks Goldman if The Death Maiden is coming to the wedding.

"Why would The Death Maiden be at the wedding?" asks Goldman.

"I don't know," says Schlots. "I figured because she's in the Bush League, you might have invited her."

"I didn't invite my entire fantasy football league to my wedding, if that's what you're asking," says Goldman.

"All right. I just figured since she made the play-offs, inviting her would be the right thing to do. A professional courtesy, if you will," says Schlots.

Goldman darts away.

1:03 P.M.

The kickoff of the wedding commences to rapt attention. Not a soul utters a word.

1:05 P.M.

Adam begins the walk down the aisle accompanied by his parents. Choral music plays in the background. Adam, inexplicably, is "shadowboxing" his way to the front of the temple. He flicks jabs, ducks and dips his head, and throws an occasional uppercut. Then he flicks some more jabs before straightening his bow tie. A number of the men in attendance are amused. A number of the women are confused.

The Goldman parents are walking down the aisle ahead of Adam. Prash attempts to bump fists with Mr. Goldman as he walks by. Mr. Goldman gives him a curious look, partially lifts his hand, but continues walking.

1:12 P.M.

Prash does his first check of his HP iPAQ for early game developments. As expected, Curtis Martin is running wild. Thind does a subtle fist pump. Kwame elbows him in the ribs.

1:17 P.M.

"The Wedding March" plays and Margaret Ming appears at the beginning of the aisle with her parents. She looks beautiful. The Mick whispers a "Bwwwongggg!" to himself. He smiles as she walks by, then he waves and takes her picture.

1:23 P.M.

Twenty minutes into the wedding, Prash rechecks his HP iPAQ. Much to his dismay, his quarterback this week, Kerry Collins, just dropped back into his own end zone, was flushed to his right by the rush, and threw a hurried 5-yard screen to Justin Fargas. It is an errant pass, however, and bounces off of Fargas's helmet. It is then intercepted by Schlots's defense. Said defense then rumbles in for a short defensive touchdown.

Six points the easy way for Schlots.

Thind lets out a "Nooooo!" The rabbi momentarily stops, and

looks at Prash over his reading glasses. Prash smiles meekly and adjusts his yarmulke.

1:35 P.M.

The rabbi pronounces Margaret and Adam "husband and wife." Adam, per Jewish wedding tradition, stomps on a glass. Lopez shouts "Olé!" while the rest of the crowd shouts "Mazel tov!"

2:00 P.M.

The guests move to the wedding reception. Prashun, Kwame, and Schlots are furiously poring over stats and tabulating scores as they walk down the receiving line. They shake hands, then re-tabulate scores near the bar. The Death Maiden has had a big day so far. Her scrubby third wide receiver, Nate Burleson, has gone berserk for 3 touchdowns.

Kwame pretends to be above this behavior, but then asks, "How am I doing?"

"Slow start."

"Anything can happen at this time of the year," says Schlots. "I could see Burleson having a big day. Random wide receivers always seem to come out of nowhere."

Kwame nods, but looks nervous.

2:01 P.M.

Lopez attempts to get involved, but gets the look-off from Vanessa. He puts his arm around his wife and sips pink lemonade.

2:30 P.M.

The bride and groom appear. They're beaming. Kwame says that it's "good to see Goldman looking so happy."

2:35 P.M.

Schlots locates a small portable television in the back of the kitchen. He tells Thind about his discovery, and the two decide to "relocate."

Without being told anything, Lopez senses what's happening. He turns to Vanessa and says, "Baby, I got to use the restroom."

He bolts through the double doors of the kitchen and finds Schlots and Thind. The three of them sit on milk crates in the back with the dishwashers, watching the 49ers–Rams game on a crappy black-and-white television, banging the side of the box from time to time when the reception gets fuzzy.

2:50 P.M.

Halftime—The boys sheepishly trickle back into the banquet room. The wedding reception forms a circle and breaks out into the traditional dancing of the "Hava Nagila." Schlots recognizes this song from hockey games, and gets very into it. With two hands he lifts his yarmulke off and on, off and on, as if it were a top hat. Then, in a fit of dancing ecstasy, he hurls himself into the middle of the circle and begins doing the Russian squat-kick dance.

TOP FIVE MOST-PECULIAR SONGS PLAYED AT SPORTING EVENTS

1. "YMCA"—song celebrating young, gay love
2. "Hava Nagila"—song celebrating Jews
3. "Doctor Who"—song celebrating a British guy who ran around in a long scarf and disappeared in a phone booth
4. Garry Glitter's "Rock and Roll Part 2"—leads to mindless, primal shouting
5. "Macarena"—We have found no explanation in Western civilization for how this song became socially acceptable, let alone popular

3:02 P.M.

Schlots, Thind, Kwame, and The Mick pick at their entrees of salmon and chicken cordon bleu. From time to time, one of them darts into the kitchen. The maid of honor is delivering her speech and giggling a great deal. No one is listening to her. Schlots begins to surreptitiously stuff silverware into the pockets of Prashun's suit jacket, which hangs on the back of his chair. Thind's jacket sags under the weight of several table settings of silver.

3:08 P.M.

Kwame returns to the table with an excited look in his eye. "Fellas, Brian Griese is going nuts. You gotta check this out." In one fluid movement Schlots, Thind, and The Mick bolt from their chairs. Lopez looks to Vanessa for permission to join them.

She shakes her head. "It's a wedding. You're not going anywhere. You're staying with me." Lopez bows his head, and stabs at a droopy piece of salmon.

3:10 P.M.

Lopez tosses his napkin onto his plate and stands. "Vanessa, it's the play-offs. I really have no other choice." He quickly darts through the swinging double doors of the kitchen.

3:12 P.M.

Thind, Schlots, Lopez, Kwame, and The Mick, are sitting on milk crates, taking in the game. Predictably, Schlots is starting Brian Griese for no particular reason. Things are suddenly looking very good for Schlots.

Thind scours his printouts of his and Schlots's rosters. He makes some notes. Adds a few numbers. Then looks up at the screen in shock. He's realized that he's fallen behind Schlots. He orders the first of many drinks.

3:17 P.M.

Prash reemerges to snag his third pink cosmopolitan. He's well liquored. A sly smile spreads across his face as his eyelids droop. An attractive woman walks by, and he paws at her shoulder. She shrugs him off, rolls her eyes, and walks away. He flings a carrot at her that misses wide-left.

3:18 P.M.

"This is the Thindianapolis Colts' year. Redemption is mine. Nothing can stop us. Not Schlots and his rope-a-dope antics. And not some dopey girl," says Thind. "The Super Bowl is mine."

3:19 P.M.

"Settle down, you Sikh fuck," says an amused Lopez.
"Did you just call me a sick fuck? What's your problem?"
"No, I called you a Sikh fuck, not a sick fuck."
"Oh. Well, I'm Hindu, not Sikh. Get your facts straight."
"What's the difference between Sikh and Hindu?"
"I have no idea."
They both laugh, clink glasses, and pound down another shot. Prashun wipes his mouth with the back of his tuxedo sleeve.

4:11 P.M.

Adam and Margaret make their grand departure for their honeymoon. On his way out the door, Adam is greeted one last time by the

Bush Leaguers. Prashun informs Adam that his squad, Team Goyim, despite not having an opponent, got pulverized. Adam doesn't the least bit care.

Prashun finds this hard to believe. "How can that not bother him?"

"You'll understand someday," says Lopez.

"Don't bet on it," Schlots says.

4:15 P.M.

The reception ends and the boys trickle back into the kitchen.

At long last Thind vanquishes the ghost Fat Minnesota Guys. He pats every dishwasher on the back and thanks them for supporting the Thindianapolis Colts.

Schlots did his best to rope-a-dope a win, but come play-off time, the elite players tend to step up big. Thind is on cloud nine. Schlots is just happy to have scored some free food and drink.

In the other play-off game, Kwame was unceremoniously dumped by The Death Maiden. Typically, he's mocked as a "girly-man" by The Mick. But one of the closely held secrets in the Bush League all season was that The Death Maiden had a good team. Everyone knew it. So Kwame gracefully bows out. And sets up the battle of the sexes in the Super Bowl.

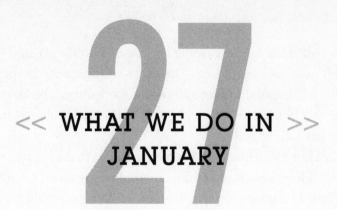

<< WHAT WE DO IN >>
JANUARY

FOR FANTASY FOOTBALL MANAGERS JANUARY IS A TIME OF transition. Some men return to their families. Some lose contact with the rest of the Bush League. And some just hibernate.

For those of us who live and breathe fantasy football, it's a sad time.

A time of mourning.

A time of regret.

But there's always next year. The Goldfish Ceremony is a mere one hundred and eighty days away, and much planning, hashing, strategizing, and pointless machinating must be done. Yes, it's true, the Bush League isn't always in-season.

But it's never far from our minds.

ONWARD AND UPWARD

The most active Bush League manager in January is Prashun Thind. The man never stops. Fantasy football, his true love, is but one chapter in his nonstop fantasy sports experience.

"Fellas, great season. The Schmuck Cup looks great in my office—absolutely beautiful. But no rest for the weary. I got a great fantasy basketball league shaping up. Anyone up for playing?"

Prashun is met by silence. The other managers are burned out, fried from five months of intense fantasy footballing. The idea of following the box scores of Stephon Marbury and Robert "Tractor" Traylor has little appeal.

"Okay, not much interest," Prashun responds to the league's wall of silence. "How about something more low impact? I have Phil Mickelson in a great fantasy golf league. If anyone would be up for joining in, I think Ernie Els is still available. Anyone?"

Nothing.

"Okay, last chance. Guys, I'm just trying to help here. Not holding a gun to your heads. So is there any interest in joining my NASCAR fantasy league? It's the latest and greatest in fantasy sports."

Finally, Prashun gets a response.

"Thindy Infante," says The Mick, "what on earth is an Indian guy doing in the world of NASCAR? That's like Goldman going to Bible camp. You actually like NASCAR?"

"I love it. Thindy Infante is a card-carrying member of NASCAR nation. I got my tickets to Daytona already. There are black rodeo riders, right? So what's wrong with an Indian guy grooving on NASCAR?"

"If you say so."

"So, what do you think? Wanna join my league?"

"Nope."

His efforts to expand the Bush League's fantasy sports horizons have once again fallen on deaf ears. So Thind soldiers on. He finds new leagues, new friends, and new antagonists. He simply can't stop marching.

NO REST FOR THE WEARY

While Thind quickly moves on from one fantasy sports season to the next, others opt to stay focused. They roll up their shirtsleeves and immediately start planning for August.

"No rest for the weary. That's what they say," notes Schlots.

"Is that what they say?" says The Mick.

"That's what they say."

In mid-January, both Schlots and The Mick are already scouting the upcoming NFL draft. They're also watching the latest *NFL Game of the Week* on the NFL Network, hoping to find any season-altering trends.

"You know, as effective as the Patriots offense is," says The Mick, "I couldn't tell you who any of their receivers are. It's like they have a bunch of guys from a flag-football team catching passes and scampering about."

"Personally, I like Kevin Faulk," say Schlots. "I don't know why. I just do."

In a few weeks they'll initiate their first mock drafts. They'll log onto AntSports.com and join the few other fantasy crackheads feeding their addiction.

"It looks like there's going to be tremendous depth at the running back position next season," says Schlots. "You got Steven Jackson coming down the pike. Those Jones boys—Julius and Kevin—they look nice. They look nice. You know, it might not be the worst year to be *up around the bend*, O'Brien."

"Schlots, I have no intention of being *up around the bend*. I've been studying goldfish behavior. I think I've come up with a strategy to elude Tark and Peepers."

"O'Brien, they're fish. You can't solve fish."

"Schlots, anything can be solved. The Irish Potato Famine will have a high pick next season. Bank on it."

HIBERNATION

Upon the conclusion of the season Lopez drops off the Bush League mailing list. He needs to get back to being Al the Father. He needs to circle back to his family—the wife, the kid. *It's amazing,* he thinks, *how much Oscar has grown in just these four short months!*

He feels a pang of regret.

But then he realizes that Oscar's wailing prevented him from fielding a good team. *Next year,* he thinks, *I'm fielding without a baby in tow.* But just now Al has his kid in his arms, and he couldn't care less. Well, sort of.

He's like a furry brown bear. He's stocking up for the long fantasy football off-season, acquainting himself with his den and brood, and getting ready to head into hibernation.

FINE-TUNING THE ENGINE

At the conclusion of each fantasy season, there's a brief post-mortem. A time to assess how the league went, what worked, and what didn't. Typically there is a direct correlation between poor records and finding fault with aspects of the league.

The free-agent market was unfair, the points awarded to kickers and defenses arbitrary, quarterbacks were shortchanged for passing touchdowns, or the draft was just too damn long.

It's the last gasp of Kwame's thankless job as commissioner to go over all this, sift through the vast and hidden agendas, and consider ways of tweaking or improving the rules and regulations of the Bush League. That's what he tells himself anyway.

"Bush Leaguers, I'm conducting an informal survey to get input on what to consider changing in the league rules for next season. Send me any and all thoughts if you want them heard."

"Cool. There's a bunch of things I want to address," responds The Mick.

"Thanks for doing this, Kwame," says Schlots. *"I'm putting together my list right now, and will send it to you shortly."*

"At last a voice of reason steps forward," notes Thind.

But the reality is that few, if any, changes will be made in the off-season to the Bush League. That's largely due to laziness and inertia.

Guys will talk about submitting ideas, and discussing them with Kwame, but they won't get around to it.

Kwame knows all of this. He doesn't take it personally. And that's why he is—and will always be—the Bush League commissioner.

PARTING SHOTS

"You guys can go to hell," The Bitter Drafter writes before disappearing for six months.

"Guys, I'll be back to take your money next year," writes The Death Maiden.

"Next year we'll be ready!" chirps the Two-Headed Hydra. *"We swear!"*

EPILOGUE: TAKING A KNEE

The final ritual in the Bush League off-season is the effort to finally break free of fantasy football. Each year, amid the biting January cold, guys reflect on the experience and wonder whether it's all worth it.

So much time and money spent.

So much frustration.

So little achieved.

Adam Goldman feels like every fantasy football season should be his last. He's now a married man, he's undoubtedly facing a barrage of husbandly and household duties with the recently renamed Margaret Ming-Goldman,[27] and he still needs to finish his residency.

In short, there's more to life than fantasy football. Or so he thinks.

"Boys, I've been doing a lot of thinking, and have come to the conclusion that I've played my last Bush League season. I'm taking a knee. I'm out."

"Come on, Adam," Kwame says. "Everyone wants you back in. We all have our lives outside fantasy football, but little without it."

---

27. Never has there been a more awkward hyphenated surname.

"Probably true, but I think I've had it. I'm forcing myself to do this. I gotta get out," says Goldman. "It's been fun, boys."

"He'll be back," says Lopez to Kwame. "Like a homing pigeon, he'll be back."

Adam wants to move on. To cast free the chains of fantasy football. But Lopez is right. Goldman will be back.

They'll all be back.

Every last one of them will return to the Bush League.

It is, like gravity, an inevitable pull that cannot be fought.

We will play fantasy football until we die.